DATE DUE

DEMCO 38-296

The American Ritual Tapestry

Recent Titles in
Contributions in Sociology

The Temptation to Forget: Racism, Anti-Semitism, Neo-Nazism
Franco Ferrarotti

Critical Theory and Political Possibilities: Conceptions of Emancipatory
Politics in the Works of Horkheimer, Adorno, Marcuse, and Habermas
Joan Alway

Demographic and Structural Change: The Effects of the 1980s on American
Society
Dennis L. Peck and J. Selwyn Hollingsworth, editors

Family, Women, and Employment in Central-Eastern Europe
Barbara Łobodzińska, editor

Constructing the Nation-State: International Organization and Prescriptive
Action
Connie L. McNeely

New Poverty: Families for Postmodern Society
David Cheal

Housing Privatization in Eastern Europe
*David Clapham, Jozsef Hegedus, Keith Kintrea, and Ivan Tosics, with Helen
Kay, editors*

Women, Work, and Gender Relations in Developing Countries: A Global
Perspective
Parvin Ghorayshi and Claire Bélanger, editors

Emerging Organizational Forms: The Proliferation of Regional
Intergovernmental Organizations in the Modern World-System
James Hawdon

Alienation, Ethnicity, and Postmodernism
Felix Geyer, editor

Cultural Practices and Socioeconomic Attainment: The Australian Experience
Christopher J. Crook

The Civic and the Tribal State: The State, Ethnicity, and the Multiethnic
State
Feliks Gross

THE AMERICAN RITUAL TAPESTRY

Social Rules and Cultural Meanings

Edited by MARY JO DEEGAN

Contributions in Sociology, Number 122

Greenwood Press
Westport, Connecticut • London

Riverside Community College
Library
4800 Magnolia Avenue
Riverside, CA 92506

E 169.04 .A5285 1998

The American ritual tapestry

Library of Congress Cataloging-in-Publication Data

The American ritual tapestry : social rules and cultural meanings /
    edited by Mary Jo Deegan.
      p.   cm. — (Contributions in sociology, ISSN 0084–9278 ; no.
122)
    Includes bibliographical references (p.   ) and index.
    ISBN 0–313–30465–3 (alk. paper)
      1. United States—Social life and customs—1971– . 2. Popular
culture—United States—History—20th century.   3. Rites and
ceremonies—United States—History—20th century.   4. Social
interaction—United States—History—20th century.   I. Deegan, Mary
Jo, 1946– . II. Series.
E169.04.A5285   1998
306′.0973—dc21   98–14232

British Library Cataloguing in Publication Data is available.

Copyright © 1998 by Mary Jo Deegan

All rights reserved. No portion of this book may be
reproduced, by any process or technique, without the
express written consent of the publisher.

Library of Congress Catalog Card Number: 98–14232
ISBN: 0–313–30465–3
ISSN: 0084–9278

First published in 1998

Greenwood Press, 88 Post Road West, Westport, CT 06881
An imprint of Greenwood Publishing Group, Inc.

Printed in the United States of America

The paper used in this book complies with the
Permanent Paper Standard issued by the National
Information Standards Organization (Z39.48–1984).

10 9 8 7 6 5 4 3 2 1

To Andre Norton

Who inspired me as a child with her adventures in outer space,
continues to fascinate me with new sagas, and
generously shares her friendship today

Contents

Preface

American rituals are fascinating: Sometimes they are chaotic, but they are almost always meaningful. This anthology emerged from the shared interests of a number of my present students, former students, and colleagues. I owe a debt of gratitude to the students in a number of classes between 1989 and 1997 who have read my earlier work on rituals and discussed their own ritual ideas and experiences. I continue to admire and respect the late Victor Turner who was my professor in 1972–1973 and the late Erving Goffman who allowed me to criticize and discuss his work with him for a number of years, especially from 1978–1980. The University of Nebraska-Lincoln and Dean Brian Foster have funded several of my travels involving ritual studies, and the International Affairs Program there, directed by Merlin Lawson, has been generous as well.

Greenwood Press has been a stalwart ally on this and other projects since the early 1980s. Dr. James T. Sabin of the Greenwood Publishing Group guided this particular book to its completion and his support was greatly appreciated.

My greatest debt is to my brilliant, critical, and peripatetic life partner, Michael R. Hill, who accompanies me on my ritual explorations, drives all over Europe with great zest, and helps me in so many ways that I cannot enumerate them all. My late mother Ida May Scott Deegan visited dozens of ritual locations and attended hundreds of ritual events with me as a child and as an adult, and these events created rich memories and experiences over many decades.

I

Introduction

1

Weaving the American Ritual Tapestry

Mary Jo Deegan

Rituals create a community stage for cultural experience, symbols, and values. They can generate, change, destroy, and maintain meaning, and in the U.S.A.[1] they can engage in these processes simultaneously and rapidly. The patterns emerging from this complex, dynamic fabric of life create a tapestry with recognizable and meaningful images and symbols. These patterns are sometimes formed by the replication of rules and values in vastly different settings with different types of participants. Sometimes these patterns generate an echo reinforcing each other; sometimes the patterns meld into a collage with a barely discernible or unexpected pattern for social behavior (Deegan 1989a, 154–67). The American ritual tapestry, the subject of this book, is woven from these echoes and clashes, and everyday life usually makes sense, despite the fact that it is sometimes alienating and unstable.

American rituals emerge from a hyper-modern society (Giddens 1990), a world where multiple rules and meanings flourish in a fast-paced, new version of modernity. A hyper-modern characteristic of American rituals is their ability to be transplanted in other cultures where they can grow and adapt with the rapidity they exhibit in the U.S.A. Some people in other countries find American rituals dangerous and destabilizing while other people in these same societies actively adopt and change these rituals to generate a new ritual tapestry, one that is sometimes quite different and sometimes quite similar to our own.

For example, I have traveled in many countries[2] in the 1990s—Costa Rica, England, Germany, the Netherlands, and Italy, to name a few—and have found a McDonald's fast-food franchise in each country. This is often both a welcome sight and quite alienating: It is good to feel "at home" in a strange land, but I travel precisely to get away from "home" and to have new experiences. Thus I try to avoid such American franchises but I, like billions of other people, often find myself low on funds or energy and glad to see those golden arches. McDonald's and other identifiable settings for American rituals quickly adapt to an international marketplace and help generate a worldwide ritual tapestry emerging from the U.S.A.

Many contemporary scholars argue that our society is postmodern and, therefore, capable of endless possible interpretations and meanings. Even individual and arbitrary meanings are possible. Postmodernists assume that contemporary society is structurally different and disconnected from the modern worldview. Life in postmodern societies is rootless, fragmented, manipulated, and different from appearances. Rationality is dead and a false goal.[3]

I believe this convoluted and agonizing theory of meaning and action is inaccurate and is a potential source of alienation and anomie (Deegan 1989a). Rational meanings are not disconnected from everyday life, as many postmodernists suggest. As complex and sometimes bizarre as American rituals are, Americans find and create their culture and everyday life through ritual. If I did not believe that other people's behavior was meaningful and capable of being understood, I would not write this book or observe social behavior. I believe, along with George Herbert Mead (1934), that we have the capacity to take the role of the other (Deegan 1992). Society and the collective others who comprise it are not postmodern or beyond rational understanding or disconnected from the past.

All the chapters included in this book employ a theory called "critical dramaturgy."[4] A few terms from this perspective are defined next to make our common framework clearer, and each chapter builds on this shared background.

CRITICAL DRAMATURGY: A THEORY OF AMERICAN RITUAL DRAMAS

Critical analysis reveals that hyper-modern life, in direct contrast to nonmodern and traditional societies, is increasingly organized on the basis of theatrical metaphors that are controlled by anonymous and powerful elites. A dramaturgical society is "one in which the technologies of social science, mass communication, theater and the arts are used to manage attitudes, behaviors, and feelings of the population in modern mass society" (Young and Massey 1978, 78). These technologies provide images of equality, democracy, and service while advancing the vested interests of the elite.

The structure of everyday life in a dramaturgical society is manipulated by elites who control symbols and images of the self and community that are incorporated into ritual events and products. An emancipatory community based on democratic control could be achieved, however, and a step toward enacting this ideal would be understanding how inequality and alienation are incorporated into rituals and how human experiences emerge from them.

In 1989, after many years of work,[5] I analyzed this emancipatory potential in two major forms of American rituals. One type (Schutz 1967, 1971) is a participatory ritual involving everyday people in its performance. Examples include ice cream socials, church dinners, amateur sporting events, picnics, poker parties, and community dances. The rituals are often organized through institutions such as voluntary associations, families, churches, and schools. The other type is a media-constructed ritual involving professional performers supported by corporate patterns of control, marketing, and funding. Examples include music videos, fanzines, popular magazines, television series, films, and compact disks. Combinations of these two ritual types are particularly potent and are capable of generating deep emotions, if not considerable frenzy, for example, rock concerts, professional sports matches, and Star Trek conventions.

More formally, participatory rituals (1) involve face-to-face, participatory interaction; (2) are socially situated in a matrix of roles, social statuses, institutions, and culture; and (3) are organized by a set of rules for ritual action. Media-constructed rituals are (1) constructed by professionals who work in the mass-media industry; (2) products that are presented to an audience; and (3) organized by a set of rules for portraying ritual action (Deegan 1989a, 4–5).

American rituals of both types are intended to be part of leisure life, and, therefore, they are seen as less serious than work. They generate a typical experience (Schutz 1971) called "fun." Fun, I argue, is a product of hyper-modern society.[6] Specifically, fun emerges from enjoyable experiences that are generated in contexts of discrimination and technological control (Deegan 1989a, 26). Fun has the appearance, but not the reality, of playfulness (Deegan 1989a, 28). Fun, as I (Deegan 1989a, 26) state elsewhere:

allows the individual to be partially incorporated in the group and because of the presence of considerable alienation, this partial tie is strongly held and defended. "Good times," the events associated with fun, maintain inequality and alienation because they create the appearance of an escape from these very problems.

This attachment to a partial release from everyday life is "seductive"; it is an alluring but dissatisfying experience (see chapter 6). Alienated individuals feel that "good times" are necessary because these situations feel so much better than everyday life. Because fun is one of the few alternatives to work in the U.S.A., and because it generates partially enjoyable experiences, it is strongly defended by everyday people. Thus alienated persons insist on the perpetuation of fun, and they are highly resistant to any critique of the structural inequalities incorporated in the processes that generate their good times.

Fun in the U.S.A. is considered a dimension of private life and is insulated, therefore, from public control or critique. The seductive character of fun emerges from its predictable capacity to generate short-lived, incomplete escapes from mundane routine. In the process, it simultaneously strengthens and reproduces the core oppressions and repressions of everyday life. Jurgen Habermas (for example, 1987) has explored extensively the disconnections of the life-world and the social system, or the separation of everyday life from the larger institutional apparatus. He advocates "communicative competence," a skilled participation in social decision making, as a mechanism to connect the individual with the larger social group. I believe fun is a mechanism that keeps these two parts from connecting and makes large social issues incomprehensible to the everyday person. Thus people resist ending social injustice because they fear that something that gives them meaning and pleasure, "fun," will be taken from them as the "price for justice."

American fun, nonetheless, provides its consumers with ritual experiences that are simultaneously attractive and alienating. This double-edged feature characterizes most media-constructed rituals in the U.S.A. Fun-producing rituals result when the "core codes," or pervasive and significant rules organizing everyday life in America (discussion follows), are imported into ritual events that could otherwise generate "play," community renewal, and culturally significant releases from the oppressive and repressive dimensions of our society.

Indeed, this mechanism has progressed so far that the delightful liminal joy of undifferentiated "play" that is not structured along sex and class lines or unbounded by temporal precision or bureaucratized rules for "scoring" is a puzzlement to many, if not most, Americans. The increasing pressure to "have fun" in American society has all but pushed genuine play to the peripheries of experience.

Hyper-modern life in the U.S.A., and the rituals that give it meaning, is driven by "core codes" of oppression and repression that order a wide range of cultural patterns, from fleeting, face-to-face interactions to enduring, large-scale social institutions. Four core codes (sex, class, bureaucratization, and the commodification of time), in particular, give recognizable contours to modern American rituals and contribute to the seductive character of fun. They structure everyday life and the larger social system.

Rituals in traditional societies use anti-structural rules, guidelines that are different from everyday rules, to order action and meaning during the extraordinary period of activity. Rituals in hyper-modern society, however, mix anti-structure and structure to attach emotions and social meaning to everyday rules of oppression and repression. The global Americanization of culture, moreover, is accelerated through market forces developed by international corporations. At stake here is not the simple merchandizing of fun, but the simultaneous mass export of the "core codes" that make fun attractive.

Thus the anthropologist Victor Turner (1969) portrays traditional societies as generating a "communitas" experience through anti-structure, an experience wherein each member's essential humanity is recognized and shared. Communitas helps a person make sense of everyday life and create human bonds despite a flawed, mundane reality. Everyone in a traditional society has a structured role in the community that may or may not be equal to others and that is frequently categorized by sex, kin, and age. Everyone in a traditional society has a role in community rituals, however, and in this sense, everyone belongs to the group. In hyper-modern societies, however, many people are excluded from fun rituals if they are the "wrong" sex, race, class, or social status. Although I originally focused on four core codes—class, sex, modern use of time, and bureaucracy—many more exist; for example, race, heterosexuality, age, terrorism, international hegemony, and religion. Several authors in this anthology broaden my original analysis by examining some of these other core codes. I also analyzed six rituals in my book *American Ritual Dramas* (Deegan 1989a), and this anthology greatly expands the number of rituals examined.[7]

A Note on American Rituals and Social Change

American rituals are extremely flexible and can appear and disappear quite rapidly. Some changes are so ephemeral that they are "fad rituals," referring to their passing interest and unstable ties to American life. Some rituals are linked to fundamental social institutions, however, and they are rapidly changing, too. These changes affect the very foundation of American society. Agnes Riedmann (chapter 11) examines a wide variety of social changes that are reflected in the funeral ceremony. This previously sacred event located family boundaries, patterned grief, and brought together community mourners. But what is the family and who are the central mourners after a divorce? If family definitions become unclear, then the process of mourning becomes unclear, and the general community is unsure whom to comfort and when.

The topic of massive social change runs through most of the anthology and I will mention, here, only a few changing definitions of the sacred in American ritual. Anthony J. Blasi's (chapter 9) analysis of American religions reflects another fundamental shift in conceptualizing moral and "proper" behavior: Making religious events more fun and entertaining makes religious events more profane. Both Yochanan Altman (chapter 7) and I (chapter 6) discusses Disney theme parks, but neither of us discusses the many, many weddings (traditionally, a religious, community-based ritual) that are performed there. Disneyland wedding parties can hire "Mickey Mouse" and "Goofy" to attend their nuptials, which may begin with a "pumpkin chariot" drawn by white horses, like some bizarre, expensive (paid by a real person and not a fairy godmother), Cinderella fairy tale caricature. These changing religious ceremonies and symbols are part of the very large ritual tapestry that the authors explore.

This anthology is an invitation to think about the American ritual tapestry and its growing complexity. One organizing thread throughout this book is the concept of core codes, and the book begins with an analysis of racism, a particularly invidious core code with an oppressive set of rules.

RACISM AS A CORE CODE IN AMERICAN RITUAL

The pervasive and powerful pattern of racism is explored by the first two authors. Todd J. Schroer (chapter 2) examines the hyper-modern forms of racism found in white nationalists' media-constructed rituals. These groups draw on modern technology to find a widely scattered and anonymous audience to disseminate their formulaic hate and fear. Schroer accurately shows how this old formula with new technology expands the more limited formats of face-to-face, participatory rituals such as those found in the Ku Klux Klan prior to the 1970s.

Michael R. Ball (chapter 3) examines the core code of racism with a philosophical analysis of evil and its connection to the American dream. He argues that the fit between larger American values and racism makes it hard to change or eradicate this underside of American life. Sports such as wrestling and video games employ a simplistic framework of "good vs. evil" that justifies eradicating and destroying anything or anyone that is considered evil, while the intolerance and violence precipitated by such a worldview is defined as "good."

Racism is, of course, aided and abetted by another form of group oppression and repression: sexism, our next topic.

SEXISM AS A CORE CODE IN AMERICAN RITUAL

Thomas C. Calhoun, Rhonda Fisher, and Julie Ann Harms Cannon (chapter 4) tackle a theoretically challenging form of sexism: amateur stripping. These bawdy acts occur with the cooperation of women who wish to disrobe in front of men drinking in a bar. This ritualized behavior poses problems of determining how liberated these young women are. How much fun is occurring and for whom? And how much change has occurred in women's social status in our hyper-modern society when women choose to be ogled and, potentially, physically endangered by strange men who lust after them? Do these women challenge repressive norms of self presentation, or is this just typical pornographic behavior (Deegan and Stein 1978)? These authors challenge the reader to confront sexism, which, like most sexism, is supported by many people in our larger society and condemned by many others.

A good example of the tapestry linking what are apparently different rituals is found in another form of female ogling: the Miss America Pageant. Lisa K. Nielsen (chapter 5) analyzes this event that results in the annual selection of the one woman who is "our ideal" American beauty. This contest creates a "beauty code" that differs from the amateur stripping "beauty code." Although the competition tries to broaden its image as an enjoyable experience for the contestants and a scholarship resource for beautiful women, it is, like most American games, a process of picking winners and losers.

Many American women participate in such beauty contests, and it is an important female *rite de passage* in our hyper-modern society. I was no exception. I "ran" in the local Miss Junior Miss when I was 15 years old in 1962. I remember being asked about a visit by Mrs. Chiang Kai-shek, the wife of the then-head-of-state of Taiwan. Although I knew nothing about her, I recall making a critical comment about the U.S. government's propaganda machine. I distinctly remember that the judges' eyebrows almost rose higher than their hairlines in shock, and I walked out thinking something like this: "Well I blew that—but I do think her visit is an arranged hype. Such is life." Undaunted by this experience, I also "ran" in the Miss St. Joseph (Michigan) contest in 1965 when I was 19 years old and was the oldest of about 25 participants. No one thought it was anything but a beefcake (Deegan 1989a, 14) contest, and the dramaturgically earnest and sweet contestants who thought they had a chance to win were incredibly "bitchy" backstage (Goffman 1959). The rest of us, who were not serious contestants, were not "dramaturgically nice"; we sat and laughed in the gallery after we were each rejected and saw all but one dramaturgically nice contestants rejected.

I also recall picketing the Miss Kalamazoo (Michigan) contest in 1971 after my "consciousness was raised" as a feminist, sociology graduate student at Western Michigan University (Deegan 1993). I was part of the Kalamazoo Women's Liberation Group, and we marched in front of the doors and tried to get arrested. The policeman on duty, however, just laughed at us (and later with us) and it was far from a confrontation.

I add my amusing and now-distant memories about beauty contests because some types of American rituals (maybe not the ones discussed here) permeate all our lives and shape our sense of self and society in fundamental ways. These rituals are shared increasingly throughout the world because of the international corporate sponsors who export American rituals, core codes, and fun. Lisa K. Nielsen argues that such sponsorship is necessary to continue such contests, but, of course, the question is whether we should continue them. Another question is whether any "American" controls international corporations and their spread of American-style rituals.

Unlike Nielsen, I see beauty contests as part of the American ritual tapestry including meet/meat market rituals in singles bars and the commodification of women's sexuality (Deegan 1989a). An interesting and important challenge to my position, however, is the support of beauty contests by physically disabled women. They argue that when they compete in beauty contests, they create a new physical standard of beauty and thereby participate in a liberating ritual (Deegan and Brooks 1985). Weaving the American ritual tapestry is an ever-changing and complex process, a theme we explore further.

AMERICAN RITUALS AND GLOBALIZATION

American rituals are incredibly powerful. The seductive character of American fun is evident in the rapid and widespread distribution of American movies, novels, films, television series, dress, and images (my chapter 6). "The Americanization of Ritual Culture" was the topic of an international conference that I attended in 1992 in Wales, but to my dismay—and surprise—I discovered a largely uncritical enthusiasm among this group of predominantly European experts. I had read the writings of hundreds of international experts before attending this meeting, and I had gained a sense of a large critical mass in many nations that opposed the influx of American culture. This perception was modified by this event and by my six trips to Europe between 1991 and 1997.

These trips all indicated an increasing Americanization process in dress, language, symbols, media, and everyday interactions. I had visited a number of European countries in 1971 and 1973 for approximately one month on each trip. The changes initiated between the 1970s and the 1990s, moving from more local and traditional food, dress, and popular culture to a more Americanized culture, were striking. Although European culture is flourishing and many Americanization processes are merely superficial changes, many of these alterations are more deeply embedded.

What does it mean, for example, that my life partner and I spent an entire day driving on the German autobahn (in March 1997), in an

American-franchised rental car and hearing American popular music from the 1970s at every rest stop, including the bathrooms and restaurants? It is quite possible today for an American tourist in Germany to pay for an "authentic" German experience on a bus tour, complete with "authentic" German music, while Germans are driving on the same roads in their own automobiles and listening to American music. The bus tour is an American participatory ritual that makes Germany fun to visit while insulating the Americans from the German experience which echoes American rituals. Such contradictions are exponentially possible.

Again reflecting on my own experiences, my mother took eight European bus tours in the 1960s and 1970s and filled stacks of photograph albums with images from these visits. She enjoyed these participatory rituals immensely and they generated some of her happiest memories. She recently died and it gives me pleasure to know how she loved these trips. Simultaneously, she never learned a foreign language; stayed in American international hotels; traveled in largely affluent, white tourist groups; and never took a tour for the disabled when she became increasingly physically limited. Her daily life on these tours was bureaucratically organized from dawn to dusk, with "scheduled free times," and she sometimes could not remember which countries she visited without looking at a formal schedule of where she had been and what she had done.

Although my mother was not wealthy and saved assiduously to afford these trips, she traveled with people who were considerably wealthier than she was. I know she would have been gracious to people who waited on her or whom she met in various countries, if she were aware of them. Thus I can easily see her being in a noisy group, an indistinguishable part of an "American" group invading public and private spaces of "native" others, and oblivious to the relative amount of money she had compared to others in these countries. In other words, she was a typical colonial tourist.

American rituals are attractive internationally because they emerge from and help create a hyper-modern society. More stable, traditional societies, especially in Europe which has many hyper-modern characteristics, can adapt quickly to American rituals. American rituals are often "glamorous," "amorphous," and easily adapted to local rituals. This amoeba-like quality is clear in the case of Disneyland Paris (DLP), where the "sure-fire" Disney formula looked like it was headed for disaster in its first three years. But DLP has survived, despite its American smiles and ethnocentrism.

Yochanan Altman (chapter 7) is fascinated by the transplantation and ultimate transformation of the American Disney theme parks, into the European, specifically the French, culture. He has observed Disneyland Paris (DLP) periodically from its opening in 1992 until the present and charts the path of this amusement juggernaut in this and other writings

(Altman 1995; Altman and Jones 1993). His dense and thoughtful analysis of "core code clusters" or overlapping and reinforcing core codes, that he defines and applies here, shows the complications and powerful images and changes introduced through such a "simple" entertainment. The globalization of American core codes can be problematic, like the beginning of DLP, or easily accepted, like Disney Tokyo.

Altman criticizes the "infantilization" of adults that occurs at DLP; a sterling example of this process was documented by a newspaper columnist, Richard Christianson (1997). He attended Disney World as a senior citizen and feared being an anomaly at this child-centered theme park. He was greeted, however, by a ticket taker who enthused: "We have no senior citizens here. We just have big boys and little boys and big girls and little girls." Like other good boys, Christianson did not criticize (or praise) this treatment. He just paid his "$40.81 full adult fare" and accepted the fact that there was no accommodation for the fixed income of most seniors.

Another child-oriented ritual is anchored in the mythic figure of Santa Claus. Santa is one of the most central figures in Americans' celebration of the Christmas holiday. Although Santa is a complex image manipulated by capitalists, many Americans view criticism of him as mean-spirited and "Scrooge-like." Sharon K. Larson (chapter 8) analyzes this "hero," nonetheless, and finds Santa's underbelly an uninviting place. Professional Santas—claimed by Canada, Lapland and Norway—fuel international economies and often oppress the poor who are beguiled into buying gifts they cannot afford for their children.

In contrast to the anti-liminal use of Santa Claus that is so characteristic today, L. Frank Baum, the creator of the Oz fantasy, was fascinated with Santa Claus, a liminal character in his American fairy tales (Deegan 1989a, 129–48). Baum (1902) even explained the "birth" of the immortal Claus in fairyland in *The Life and Adventures of Santa Claus*. Santa attended Princess Ozma of Oz's birthday party in *The Road to Oz* (Baum 1909). Baum celebrated Santa, moreover, in his own Christmas rituals at home. This "Ozzy" appreciation continues in today's participatory celebrations in the International Wizard of Oz Club and is reported in its mass media outlet, *The Baum Bugle* (Tobias 1996). Thus a ritual tapestry of Santa Claus weaves through our large commercial and international corporate enterprises as well as in our more intimate, liminal celebrations based on Oz.

Although there may be "sacred" or religious dimensions to popular, secular figures such as Santa Claus or Disney characters, some rituals are intentionally (Schutz 1971) religious and oriented to sacred symbols. Two of these overtly religious situations are analyzed next.

AMERICAN RITUALS AND THE SACRED IN HYPER-MODERN SOCIETY

American churches and ministers compete with a secular society that promises fun and meaning through popular culture. Anthony J. Blasi (chapter 9) examines how this competition permeates formerly traditional religious activities. The once-serious pursuit of the sacred is increasingly mixed with fun to draw an audience. Thus the anti-structural rules of traditional religions increasingly incorporate core codes from everyday life, especially bureaucratic rules. The anti-structure of religious rituals in America can now include, for example, Broadway-style musicals and performance areas rather than altars. Blasi examines the pursuit of good times within religious institutions and by their leaders.

This participatory dimension is complemented by the vast media industry of religious television, radio, and compact discs with their casts of professional singers and actors. Thus many people see a movement of the sacred into secular settings such as films and national holidays (Bellah 1970), but Blasi is examining the vital movement in the opposite direction: the entry of secular functions and experiences into sacred rituals. He argues that religion as play challenges the core codes and is anti-structural.

Sacred issues are addressed, too, in liminal adventures on the *Witch World* where mythic struggles between the gods of another planet are dramatized. This fantastic world emerges from the imagination of a great American storyteller, Andre Norton, whose role parallels that of storytellers in traditional societies. She employs many myths, histories, legends, novels, and fairy tales to recount stories of courage and adventure, often with female protagonists. Norton explores the boundaries of danger and adventure that can be conquered despite the multiple disadvantages of being poor, lonely, female, disinherited, or powerless. I call this layering of outsider statuses "multi-liminality," and it serves to heighten drama and heroic accomplishments. Norton's faith in the human spirit and the power of good to win over evil articulates the dreams of her millions of readers.

One book in this series, Norton's *The Year of the Unicorn* (1965), has a female heroine whom I analyzed in chapter 10 as an example of a transformed Oz formula with great sociological insights. Norton illustrates the continuation of sacred, liberating myths in a hyper-modern, secular society. This continuity is often challenged, if not broken, in our fast-paced society, and this rate of change is our next topic.

RAPIDLY CHANGING AMERICAN RITUALS

Death is one of the greatest mysteries of life and a challenge to human meanings and values. All societies have rituals surrounding the end of life, but American rituals surrounding death are particularly problematic. As a people we want our lives to mean something, and simultaneously we avoid confronting death, the ultimate test of life's meaning (Deegan 1975b). The community is supposed to honor the recently deceased and be comforted in this process, yet our funerals are often alienating, expensive, and filled with conflict. The rapidly changing American family, moreover, is often in crisis at funerals because the meaning of family and death dramatically collide.

Agnes Riedmann's (chapter 11) thoughtful and insightful analysis of her own experience as "The Ex-Wife at the Funeral" exposes these deep contradictions. She uses dramaturgical theory to discuss the rapid emergence of "teams of mourners" with competing members, definitions, locations, scripts, homes, and relationships. She defines a particular type of participatory ritual in this article: a "community production ritual." She focuses on this dramaturgical situation as a local event performed by friends and family in face-to-face interaction. Many of Erving Goffman's (1959, 1967) concepts, such as face-saving actions, role-playing, and alienation, apply to this presentation of self and other within a ritual context.

The typical American funeral is a capitalist product presented and orchestrated by professionals (Mitford 1963) in a "dramaturgical industry," a concept I define here. A dramaturgical industry combines structural rules; such as those governing bureaucracies, capitalism, and the workplace, with the management of a dramatic effect with both rational and emotional components. The funeral business, for example, manages corpses and emotions within a massive bureaucratic structure that encompasses and coordinates monuments; cemeteries; cosmeticians; morticians; funeral directors and their staff (Pine 1975); coffin makers; crematoriums; medical personnel in hospitals and morgues (Sudnow 1967); criminal investigators and police; ambulance services; insurance companies; banks; and expensive transportation. Moving corpses through public forms of transport such as airplanes and railroads and private transport such as limousines, cars, and hearses is a vast segment of the economics of funerals.

Television advertising is becoming increasingly sophisticated in packaging funerals, now selling the idea that the future corpse is responsible for its own funeral, thereby creating a new media-constructed ritual. Other aspects of this advertising are found in various brochures, pamphlets, and other print formats. Funerals as a dramaturgical industry are found in the U.S.A. and in other countries as well. Riedmann discusses an important segment of this larger participatory ritual.

Riedmann also discusses the disconcerting experience of being present at her ex-husband's funeral where many pictures were displayed to document her former husband's "most meaningful" life events. Although she was originally present at the events depicted, she was systematically removed from the pictures since she was "divorced" or separated from his life. A new technology makes such an erasure of family, memory, and membership even more possible: "Now, with a few clicks and strikes of a computer mouse, graphic artists can manipulate an old print or negative and erase just about anyone" ("Divorced People Get Help Erasing Their Ex" 1996). This, like most processes, is gendered. Thus divorced "girls [sic] want the man removed but the guys want the girl replaced" ("Divorced People Get Help Erasing Their Ex" 1996).

Bert Watters (chapter 12) analyzes another group undergoing rapid and often bewildering change: young Mexican-American women. Traditionally, fifteen-year-old girls in Mexico experienced a transformation ritual from child to adult in a religious and community ceremony called the "quinceañera." This *rite de passage* officially announces to her family and friends that she is a person ready to enter adult roles, particularly as a wife and mother.

In a hyper-modern society, however, this female age group is composed primarily of high school students who are far from adult roles and responsibilities. In fact, a fifteen-year-old girl who tries to act like an adult, such as becoming pregnant and then dropping out of high school, will suffer severe economic and educational disadvantages throughout her life. Although there are still very positive community responses to young mothers in Mexican-American communities, these responses are increasingly tempered by the work and gender expectations of a hyper-modern society (Horowitz 1987; Williams 1990).

What is the ideal new role for these young women? Should they postpone such celebrations? Should these ethnic, community events disappear into a "melting pot" in a hyper-modern "American" society? Should these celebrations be treasured as an important part of diversity in America? Watters poses these and other questions as important community decisions and events that challenge this Mexican *rite de passage* in an American context.

CONCLUSION

The authors included here and the rituals they examine often pose more questions than they resolve. This open-endedness is intentional because the formation and paths of American rituals are evolving and are a product of many people's ideas, money, and commitments. One fact is clear, however: American rituals are flourishing, often changing, and powerful.

The American ritual tapestry is being woven and rewoven constantly. It is understandable and subject to community control and interpretation. Thus racism and sexism are not necessary core codes but specific rules that are maintained and elaborated through the acts and emotional experiences of millions of Americans. These issues are analyzed in white nationalists' media-constructed rituals; simplistic, hegemonic video games; beauty contests; and popular science fiction. Racism and sexism also maintain large social structures and institutions. Ideology that justifies and organizes American rituals is generated often by an elite that benefits from the maintenance of inequality and injustice. Rapid technological changes can usher in new options or strengthen old patterns of love or hatred, as well.

Old ritual symbols such as Santa Claus can be co-opted to serve the functions of international economies, or they can be renewed and invigorated through American creativity found in the imagination of writers like L. Frank Baum. Sacred life can be limited and distorted by new religious practices pursuing good times and an audience, or sacred questions can be posed by popular writers such as Andre Norton. Cultural diversity can be celebrated in song and food or erased through lack of support and organized efforts, a process that occurs today within the quinceañera ritual.

American rituals are extremely fluid, but they create our emotional lives and rational discourses. Democratic, community rituals can liberate everyday life and connect the individual to the group. American rituals need more discussion and debate; more analysis and resistance to their dramaturgic and manipulated presentations. Understanding who we are requires new rules, not a mindless return to a nonexistent, nostalgic past. Recent changes instituted by divorce, for example, have been organized primarily in a legal and economic forum for individuals who were formerly married. How do divorces affect American rituals, however? Severing ties beyond the husband and wife is now murky and fraught with unresolved conflicts and grief for the friends and family of the divorced couple. Funerals, family reunions, weddings, graduations, and holidays are all systematically affected by divorce, but the lack of consensus about how to create community and communitas on such occasions requires a group, not an individual, response. This book opens up such analyses and public questions.

NOTES

1. "U.S.A." is consistently used in this book to refer to the "United States of America." Because there are other nations that have a united states designation or structure, I do not assume there is only one "United States" or "U.S." Although the use of U.S.A. is not harmonious to some people in the U.S.A., who assume that there is only one United States, this book is intentionally oriented to a global audience.

"American" is used here to refer to the culture and everyday life of people in the U.S.A. The term "American rituals" has been accepted as an identifiable pattern by many scholars to refer to this specific population. North and South Americans are "Americans," with distinctive "North American rituals" and "South American rituals." "Americanization of culture" is also recognized as a global process connected with colonial and capitalist patterns associated with the U.S.A.

2. These travels were often partially funded with the assistance of my former Dean, John Peters; my present Dean, Brian Foster; and the University of Nebraska's Department of International Affairs Program. My thanks and appreciation to these significant resources for research.

3. Postmodernists have become exceedingly popular in American cultural studies, although they originally were discussing European experiences and societies. A good discussion of the divergent assumptions between pragmatists, which I am, and postmodernists is found in Diggins (1994). He also discusses poststructuralists who believe that the rules of society are different from previous rules, rationality, and patterns. Although I am a feminist pragmatist and Diggins is not, he establishes the important philosophical arguments that I support.

4. I also use the work of early sociologists in a framework I now call "feminist pragmatism" (for example, Deegan 1978a, 1981, 1986a, 1986b, 1987a, 1987b, 1988a, 1988b, 1988c, 1989c, 1992, 1993, 1995a, 1997). I intend to connect the classical (feminist pragmatism) and contemporary (critical dramaturgy) theories into one approach. These connections were emerging in Deegan (1992, 1995a, 1997) and in Deegan and Hill (1987, 1989). More connections between these two approaches will be made in future publications and are beyond the scope of this book. A sample of this new direction is found in chapter 10.

5. I first studied American rituals in the seminars of Victor Turner in 1972–1973. I have analyzed numerous rituals in separate publications since that time in addition to the comprehensive organization of my ideas in 1989.

6. It is, unfortunately, beyond the scope of this chapter to detail the ways in which common and often highly valued participatory rituals; including apparently innocuous events as church dinners, picnics, and small-stake poker parties, typically celebrate the core codes of oppression and repression. For further discussion, see Deegan (1989).

7. I discuss other rituals elsewhere; see bibliography for a partial list of them.

II

Racism as a Core Code in American Ritual

2

White Nationalists' Media-Constructed Rituals: The Interplay of Technology and Core Codes

Todd J. Schroer

A hooded Ku Klux Klan member ignites a cross, a television program starring Christian Identity minister Pastor Peter J. Peters calls for the death penalty for homosexuals, and a computer screen flashes a swastika with the words "White Pride World Wide!" blinking around it. These are all examples of media-constructed and participatory rituals (Deegan 1989a) developed by the white nationalist movement. These rituals rely upon the often blatant expression of white supremacy, sexism, and anti-Semitism in their makeup; they perform the function of providing members of this geographically diverse movement a sense of community and solidarity among themselves (Schroer 1993).

Because of the lack of revenue and paying jobs within the movement, most individuals involved in these rituals do so in their leisure time. They choose to spend their free time, for example, engaging in participatory rituals at Christian Identity Bible retreats and interacting with media-constructed rituals while watching racist cable or satellite television programs at home.

In this chapter, I analyze the rituals found in the white nationalist movement. Since an in-depth discussion of both types of rituals would be quite extensive, I focus on media-constructed rituals. I present the media-constructed rituals as if they were not distinct, however, since ritual types are blurring in today's society (Deegan 1989a). I briefly examine participatory rituals so that I can discuss the interaction between the two types of rituals in the last section.

METHODOLOGY

The information about the white nationalist movement I discussed here was gathered from a variety of sources. I have studied the movement intensively since 1990 and have compiled a large number of primary and secondary documents from several different areas. The majority of the primary documents come from my monitoring of the computer networks, bulletin boards, ftp (file transfer program) sites, and World Wide Web (WWW) sites used and produced by white nationalists. I have also used the computer to conduct a number of interviews with members of the white nationalist movement (Schroer 1993).

Additionally, I have acquired primary documents from some of these groups through the mail. My name is on the mailing lists for a number of these groups, and I have ordered books, tapes, and pamphlets from a variety of them. I have also acquired, through a mutual acquaintance, the entire collection of white nationalist documents that had been saved by a (now-reformed) racist skinhead. Finally, I have twice visited the Wilcox Collection at the University of Kansas-Lawrence. This remarkable archive contains documents and ephemeral materials from a wide variety of current and defunct extremist groups, and it has given me access to a large number of primary documents dating back over five decades.

MEDIA-CONSTRUCTED RITUALS IN THE WHITE NATIONALIST MOVEMENT

According to Deegan (1989a, 5), media-constructed rituals are made by professionals in the mass-media industry, presented to an audience, and organized by a set of rules for portraying ritual action (see chapter 1). Here I analyze two media-constructed rituals from the white nationalist movement by discussing how they relate to more mainstream media-constructed rituals, how they are influenced by technological change, and how they affect the movement.

WHITE NATIONALIST AND MAINSTREAM MEDIA-CONSTRUCTED RITUALS: SHARING THE CORE CODES

The media-constructed rituals produced by members of the white nationalist movement share many features with those produced by the more mainstream media. Namely, they often reflect the core codes of oppression and repression: sex, class, bureaucratization, and the commodification of time (Deegan 1989a). However, the primary codes analyzed here are racism and sexism (Deegan and Hill 1989).

In reference to race, the mass media have been scrutinized repeatedly for the content of its messages and the images it portrays. Although some advances have been made, non-whites are often underrepresented or presented in stereotypical portrayals in media representations (Bell 1992; Feagin 1992; K. A. Johnson 1991). Thus, even while engaging in a leisure-time activity such as watching television, racism is reinforced (Deegan 1989a) and influences how individuals perceive, evaluate, and treat entire categories of people (Schroer 1996).

The core codes that structure the mainstream media rituals interact with those rituals produced by white nationalists, whose rituals often exploit issues and symbols covered in the mainstream media such as affirmative action or crime. The main difference is that white nationalist rituals *blatantly* express racist and sexist aspects of issues that are presented *less obviously* in the mainstream. Because these rituals are often structured by the same underlying core codes, the ability of the white nationalist messages to resonate with large segments of the society is enhanced. This resonance can help create, reaffirm, or recruit movement sympathizers into organized white nationalist groups (Schroer 1993; Snow and Benford 1988).

TWO EXAMPLES OF WHITE NATIONALIST MEDIA-CONSTRUCTED RITUALS

White nationalist media-constructed rituals, almost by definition, contain racist imagery. The presentations, while differing slightly from group to group and over time, are very formulaic in content (Deegan and Hill 1989). In brief, their argument is that whites, while naturally superior to other groups, are being denied their fair share of societal rewards due to the scheming of powerful secret groups—usually Jewish—that control all major institutions of society with the goal of destroying the white race. This formula appears again and again in the many different cultural products produced by white nationalists. I outline and discuss two specific examples of white nationalist media-constructed rituals: the Web site of Resistance Records and Scriptures for America's audiotape ministry.

Resistance Records' World Wide Web Site

Increasingly, white nationalists use computers as tools to disseminate their messages, with the newest format that of Web sites on the Internet. Web sites can include many different forms of media and usually include a mixture of text, pictures, and colors. After making contact with the Web site, a computer user can access additional information contained within the site, as well as surf to other sites at the click of a button. White nationalists have established many Web sites, but Resistance Records' Web site is by far the most cutting edge of this new form of communication.

Resistance Records is a pro-white music corporation founded by George Eric Hawthorne in 1994 to distribute and produce racist, skinhead music. It sells tapes, CDs, and videos of white power music, as well as organizes concerts in the Detroit area. It is one of many white nationalist organizations that have entered a number of different arenas—including computers—in order to reach a new pool of potential sympathizers or customers.

The Resistance Records Web site, besides incorporating text and pictures, includes audio and video presentations. Information about Resistance Records, messages from its founder, and graphics and song clips from the latest white power releases can be accessed at the website. Additionally, all the merchandise shown can be ordered on the computer by credit card.

This Web site is a cultural product, produced by highly talented individuals. Their messages are blatantly racist and sexist and are reinforced through texts, pictures, and sound. In regard to sexism, the imagery and song titles on the many webpages are primarily violent, and texts are oriented toward young, white, male "warriors." There are no women members of the white power bands portrayed, thus there are no female stars/heroes. In fact, women are referred to only once on the entire Web site and then only in terms of the evils of race-mixing: "Without the wombs of our women, we cannot reproduce our own dwindling numbers. Race-Mixing spells death." The virtual nonexistence of female recording stars and the reduction of women to baby machines in this ritual are structured by the core code of sexism.

In contrast to the invisibility of women, images of race permeate the Web site. The texts, song titles, and sound clips are primarily about such topics as racial holy wars, the destruction of American society caused by "cancerous" nonwhites, and the threat posed by enemies bent on destroying the white race. The titles of albums and the white power bands are similarly racial. Bands such as Beserkr, Nordic Thunder, Aryan, and Rahowa (short for RAcial HOly WAr) all have names that invoke the white race and its mythical heritage.

The symbolic imagery in the Web site is also primarily racial. Graphics of crosses unique to Christian Identity are present, as well as Celtic artwork and Viking warriors. The concert videoclips include images of young white men singing/shouting "White Power" while giving the Nazi salute. Once again these images revolve around current and past symbols that are associated with racial issues and the heritage of the white race.

In sum, they offer music, videos, and information to use as enjoyment and "fun" during leisure times (Deegan 1989a). The cultural products they offer are structured by the core codes, especially racism and sexism, and reaffirm them during interactions.

The ultimate purpose of this media-constructed ritual, however, is to make money. Resistance Records is a business, and its founder, Greg Eric Hawthorne, is also the lead singer for Rahowa. He has a large financial stake in selling merchandise and promoting white power music and ideology. As long as new recruits and sympathizers (read "customers") can be found, he continues to be one of the few members of the white nationalist movement to support himself on hate.

Scriptures for America's Audiotape Ministry

Let's turn now to the other white nationalist media-constructed ritual to be examined in-depth: Scriptures for America and its audiotape ministry. Scriptures for America is a "national outreach ministry" run by the LaPorte (Colorado) Church of Christ, and headed by Christian Identity Pastor Peter J. Peters. The audiotape ministry consists of recordings of sermons delivered by Pastor Peters at his Colorado church, and number over 500. The audiotapes are continually produced, cost four dollars each, and can be bought through the mail. These media-constructed rituals concern a variety of topics but revolve around Christian Identity and are structured by the core codes of sexism and racism.

Christian Identity as a religion involves an extremely racial interpretation of the Old and New Testaments. The main beliefs are that members of the white race are the true Israelites, that only whites are descendants of Adam, and that Jews are Satanically spawned and seek to annihilate Christianity and the white race. Other, more peripheral beliefs differ slightly from church to church, but they are structured by the core codes, especially racism and sexism. The similarities in all the Christian Identity beliefs and ideas revolve around race and are portrayed as eternal God-given truths, thus using the force of God and religion to reaffirm sexism and racism as natural.

Focusing upon Pastor Peters's audiotape ministry, we gain a deeper understanding of how another white nationalist media-constructed ritual is designed and consumed. These taped sermons are awash in racist and sexist themes. Listeners are continually bombarded with messages detailing how Jews control the media and government, how the white race is in constant peril from race-mixing, and how other, less racist Christian churches are distorting the truths taught by God and Jesus.

The formula discussed earlier is once again seen in the topics covered. This time, racist and sexist interpretations of current events are intermingled with and supported by biblical quotes and references to historical events. In regard to sex, once again the main characters are white men in a continual struggle against the Other, or as Pastor Peters refers to them, "Christian Enemies." Women's roles are similar to those in biblical times: to support and obey males and to reproduce the white race.

Women are usually only discussed when referring to families, marriage, the evils of feminism, or how they need to be protected and guided by men. Once again, patriarchy is reinforced through the stereotypical portrayals of women, but more through the invisibility of women in the audiotapes.

The issue of race is much more prevalent in the audiotapes. At the core of all Christian Identity beliefs is the idea that the Bible is written only for Aryans and that they are in a struggle with the forces of Satan: the Jews. Therefore, an underlying racist message is inherent within *every* discussion about Christian Identity. Racism intimately structures each of Pastor Peters's sermons.

These two examples of white nationalist, media-constructed rituals reveal a number of important issues. First, that vastly different formats of media-constructed rituals, produced by very different racist groups, are in general only slight permutations of a common formula. Young racist skinheads and middle-aged Christian Identity followers produce rituals that contain similar formulaic messages structured by the core codes. Second, these media-constructed rituals are important because they transcend time.

The rituals are linked to the past through their incorporation of past symbols and historical events, they help frame current issues today, and as cultural artifacts, they will extend into and influence the future (Deegan 1989a). Finally, these examples reveal that white nationalists use a variety of media to present their rituals. The influence of technological advances on white nationalists' ability to produce media-constructed rituals and the number of outlets for their messages are the focus of the next section.

TECHNOLOGICAL INNOVATION AND WHITE NATIONALIST MEDIA-CONSTRUCTED RITUALS

With ever-increasing technological advances in computers and communications, the number of possible media outlets accessible to white nationalists has multiplied. Due to computerization and miniaturization, the financial costs and physical difficulty associated with creating media-constructed rituals has been greatly reduced (Schneider 1995). This has allowed white nationalists at all levels to use a variety of new channels of communication to distribute their rituals.

The important, new technological products used for communicating rituals range from answering machines to shortwave radio to computers. Answering machines, for example, allow a single individual to set up a nationwide white nationalist phone hotline. The affordability and minimal technology of telephone answering machines makes them widely used by white nationalist groups, and allows people to record messages ranging from interpretations of current events in a newscast format to calls for attacks on nonwhites.

Another example is the shortwave radio. White nationalists are increasingly turning to shortwave radio stations to broadcast their programs; at least three shortwave stations currently carry racist radio programs throughout the United States. The format of the broadcasts is often a radio talk show and occasionally includes listener and phone-in portions. The amount of airtime of the broadcasts varies, but at the high end, the three-hour program "Radio Free America" is broadcast twice a day, five days a week.

These new forms of communication are important to the white nationalist movement for a number of reasons. First, they open up new audiences to the rituals produced. Increasing numbers of people are targeted, and entirely new segments of society are hearing these messages. Computer users, radio listeners, cable and satellite television watchers, and others can now be exposed to messages directly from organized groups.

Second, the ability to access white nationalist media-constructed rituals has become much easier due to technological advances. For people interested in white supremacy, the number of access points has expanded; and, through the use of machines such as computers, they can obtain information almost instantly and relatively anonymously.

Third, the legitimacy of media-constructed rituals is also influenced by changes in technology. This has occurred not only through the increasing *quality* of white nationalist cultural products generated by computerization and desktop publishing, but also through the very *use* of high-tech forms of communication itself. Using advanced types of communication can lend an air of respectability to messages they would otherwise lack, and this legitimation is especially true of computers.

Fourth, these new avenues for disseminating messages are not fully controlled by traditional institutions, and so there are avenues for different types of messages such as those of white nationalists (Deegan 1989a). These new forms of communication are still in a state of flux, and competition is raging over who should be allowed access and what they should be allowed to portray. For example, anti-hate group organizations such as the Anti-Defamation League (ADL) and the Southern Poverty Law Center (SPLC) are calling for federal and corporate regulations to curtail racist access to computer servers and shortwave radio (ADL 1996; Tugend 1994).

Finally, the new forms of communication and the media-constructed rituals are important because they facilitate a sense of community and solidarity among white nationalists who are often geographically separated from other members of the movement. Individuals can be in contact, through these new types of communication, with individuals from all around the United States. This contact helps promote unity among members and gives them a feeling of belonging to something greater than themselves, a nationwide movement (Schroer 1993). Of course, this sense of racial community is bolstered always by creating and maintaining the nonwhite Other, revealing the flawed nature of these bonds.

THE RELATION BETWEEN MEDIA-CONSTRUCTED AND PARTICIPATORY RITUALS WITHIN THE WHITE NATIONALIST MOVEMENT

There is much overlap between the media-constructed and participatory rituals of the white nationalist movement. Applying Deegan's concepts (see chapter 1), examples of white nationalist participatory rituals include Klan cross-burnings, skinhead concerts, and attendance at Christian Identity church services. Briefly, in terms of content, the rituals are structured by the core codes and reaffirm racism and sexism during a leisure-time activity aimed at promoting community.

The blurring of the two types of rituals can be seen in a number of ways. First, many of the media-constructed rituals produced by white nationalists are recordings of participatory rituals. For example, the audiotapes available from Scriptures for America are media-constructed rituals, but they are recordings of the participatory ritual of attending church. Similarly, the white power music videos available from Resistance Records are recordings of the participatory ritual of attending a white power concert.

Second, the settings in which the media-constructed rituals are consumed may be participatory rituals. For example, listening to tapes of white power bands at a party or gathering at a friend's house to watch the latest racist cable-access television program involve the use of media-constructed rituals in participatory ways.

Finally, with the increasing use of computers to present media-constructed rituals, the interactive, participatory nature of rituals is enhanced. Increasingly, individuals can choose the parts of media-constructed rituals in which they want to participate, in their own time, and at their own pace.

The two types of rituals, while blurring, also exist within a world of rituals that interact, therefore, with each other to form new and stronger patterns. This is referred to by Deegan (1989a) as "a ritual echo." A prime example of this is the audiotape ministry of Scriptures for America. The sermons began as participatory rituals that eventually were taped and transformed into media-constructed rituals. The popularity of the audiotapes led Scriptures for America to produce many other types of media-constructed rituals: videotapes, shortwave radio programs, satellite and cable television programs, newsletters, books, and computer file transfer programs (ftp) and Web sites. These cultural products are disseminated and attract individuals to the participatory rituals now sponsored by Scriptures for America, such as the Christian Minister Seminars and the annual family oriented Bible camps.

CONCLUSION

In this chapter, I examined media-constructed rituals produced by the white nationalist movement. These rituals are structured by the core codes and are formulaic in nature. They reaffirm the patriarchal, racist character of our society and even attempt to increase it, while being presented in a format that generates fun and community feelings. White nationalist media-constructed and participatory rituals also blur and influence each other. It has been shown that they are becoming increasingly intermingled, and each type of ritual can influence the creation of new, different rituals.

Finally, technological advances have had a profound effect on the rituals produced and on their messages. New forms of communication have been invented, and older forms such as printing have become easier and cheaper to use. Technology has enhanced the creation of new types of rituals while making them more accessible and legitimate to larger segments of society. These changes have had significant effects upon the white nationalist movement and have facilitated its current resurgence in America.

3

Evil and the American Dream

Michael R. Ball

The Ku Klux Klan, the American Nazi Party, White Aryan Resistance, Aryan Nation, and skinheads were viewed as fringe groups until recently.[1] The general public viewed these groups as composed of a few badly socialized individuals whose free use of racial epithets testified to their implacable, personal problems. Perhaps some of the more extreme members of these groups actually could be provoked into violence or, in rare instances, even murder. These perceptions reflected how these groups are portrayed in our popular culture—as symbols of society's failure. The increasing numbers of these groups, however, pull them ever closer to the mainstream of politics and religion in America.

The shift of extremist groups from the periphery toward the center of political life suggests that we are not dealing with "fringe" ideas but with mainstream thought. Perhaps we are not dealing with people who engage in deviant thought and behavior, but essentially normal individuals with normal American values accepting increasingly popular norms. In fact, I contend that it is not a lack of socialization or deviant socialization that perpetuates an ideology of hate, but rather successful socialization into today's social values and rules. Using Deegan's (1989a) ritual drama theory, I identify core values and explore their pervasiveness in today's popular culture. I further discuss the nature and extent of their effect on the proliferation of hate groups.

HATE AS DEVIANCE

Traditionally, criminologists have treated hate groups in much the same way as they treat street gangs or other deviant groups. Their theories allowed little distinction between typical crime groups and those groups motivated by a high degree of ideology. In contrast to these experts, some criminologists are now examining the role of ideology in the commission of criminal acts, and these new theories are particularly relevant to a discussion of racist hate groups. Steven F. Messner and Richard Rosenfeld (1994) argue in *Crime and the American Dream* that an earlier sociologist, Robert Merton (1949), was essentially correct in his theory of innovation as an adaptation to anomie, or normlessness. Although Merton believed that money was the motivating force for individual Americans, Messner and Rosenfeld claim that it is not money, but what money can buy, that is the motivation. They contend that the main motivating force in America is the "American Dream," an amorphous image created by popular culture and realized in individual variations. It usually includes a solid job, stable family, comfortable house, leisure, security, and a prestigious lifestyle that bespeaks one's value to society. The American Dream is, of course, unattainable by most Americans, but its social value is analogous to the carrot dangled before the hungry mule. If the American Dream is the carrot, then popular culture is the stick from which it dangles.

Charles Derber (1996) holds a similar view of the modern American. He reveals that the desire for excitement emerges from mundane jobs and boring lives that are compared to a background of televised excitement and danger. When a fierce belief in individualism is stirred into this mixture, it produces individuals who have little guilt about perpetrating the most hideous acts of violence for their own pleasure. This hedonism also takes capitalist greed to the limit. The resulting behavior does not reflect a failure to socialize individuals but, instead, an oversocialization in American values of competition, individualism, and materialism. This excessive greed or "wilding" behavior is evident in both government and business. It is demonstrated in novels, television, movies, and popular music and rewarded in schools. Little wonder, then, that given such role models, Americans are increasingly pursuing personal goals with little regard for their effects on others.

DRAMATIC RITUAL AND CORE CODES

American participation in popular cultural activities assumes a ritual context when viewed as a reinforcement of norms, values, and attitudes (Chapple and Coon 1942). Erving Goffman (1967) viewed unremarkable daily routine as a ritual that provides for common cultural experiences and a basis for mutual understanding and communication. Victor

Turner (for example, 1974), unlike Goffman, studied extraordinary ritual events. Both types of ritual are found in all societies and function to increase group cohesion and identity. Deegan's (1989a) discussion of ritual analyzed American popular culture as a mixture of everyday and extraordinary events organized around "core codes" (see chapter 1 here). The core codes of capitalism and sexism are especially relevant here for the construction and maintenance of racist hate groups in the U.S.A.

Many popular cultural activities contain latent messages and support for particular ideologies that are both alienating and hateful. Thus the popular definition of enemies and combative metaphor used in football, hockey, and other sports; the frequent, spontaneous violence of hockey games; the futuristic battles on Saturday morning TV cartoons; the shoot-outs and car chases in cop movies, all support and reinforce the notion of the evil "other." These events define whom to hate and provide scripts for mobilizing that hatred. The fact that many of these activities are specifically directed toward one particular segment of the population makes them all the more powerful. For example, "macho movies" star single-minded, muscle-bound super-heroes who fearlessly use violence in pursuit of their goals. Men are also the prime viewers of televised sports that feature "life-and-death" competition and violence.

Sexism

Sexism is primarily a divisive system designed to oppress and repress certain groups while allowing others to succeed. While sexism in its purist form might be viewed as "male" vs. "female," in a broader sense, it applies to many systems of bifurcation, including "majority vs. minority," "rich vs. poor," "good vs. evil," "strength vs. weakness," "us vs. them," and so on. The core code of sexism is concerned with labeling, stereotyping, and polarizing. Ultimately, it is a system of assigning differential values to human experience.

Among other things, the sexist code promotes an intolerance of ambiguity, whether it arises from gender, race, class, age, or religion. The need to define groups runs deeply through social relations. The genderless "Pat" character on the television show *Saturday Night Live*, for example, was humorous because it touched a note of truth in most of us. It called to mind, not only the oppression of gendered social institutions, but also the individual dimension of repression evidenced by our difficulty in relating to a genderless "other." Similarly, a person's race is important, not because we are afraid of insulting someone with an inadvertent slip of the tongue, but because it calls forth stereotypes that are useful in initial interactions with people (Allport 1954).

Dichotomy is an essential element of sex codes. This was embodied in the ancient Taoist notion of *yin* and *yang*. The female *yin* is the dark, the moon, the secretive side that can only reflect the sun's light. The male *yang* is the sun, the giver of light, the truth radiating outward. If the imagery is familiar, it is because we have adopted the dichotomy of *yin* and *yang* as a metaphor for good and evil in our popular culture—but with important differences.

In Taoist philosophy, *yin* and *yang* function in perfect balance. Both are necessary for the natural functioning of the universe. In Western culture, however, the universe is set against itself: It is the task of good to overcome evil. As in the founding of American democracy, or the doctrine of "manifest destiny," a task is defined. Evil is that which prevents or delays realization of those social goals. While extensive discussion and definition of "evil" is beyond the scope of this chapter, it needs to be defined in its use here.

Biblical Evil

The U.S.A. is founded upon Judeo-Christian teachings, and—as a society—its essential understanding of evil is rooted in that tradition. It is therefore important to analyze this understanding before continuing in a sociological and anthropological context.

Old and New Testament treatments of evil are somewhat different. In the Old Testament, evil is understood as a creation of God. Evil is viewed as a natural counterbalance to the bounties God provides. Attempts are made to endure evil and to minimize its impact, but it is never suggested that evil can, or should, be destroyed (DeVries 1964, 182). In point of fact, because God visits evil upon individuals and societies for His own use, He is often noted in the Old Testament as the author of "evil" (Job 2:10; Isa. 45:7; Amos 3:6).

Although the New Testament preserves some of the *yin* and *yang* nature of evil, it assumes a predominantly moral and spiritual connotation. Evil is the wrong that people do to one another (Jas. 3:8): It is "moral badness, maliciousness, and perversity of the sinful heart" (DeVries 1964, 182). The unrepentant and perpetual doers of evil are "wicked."

The fact that biblical teachings depict God as the creator of evil leads to a philosophical contradiction that Christian theologians have been struggling with for centuries. Since the New Testament especially suggests that good and evil are contradictory notions, how can a beneficent God be responsible for the creation of evil? The philosophical study of this question (known as "theodicy") traditionally takes several tacks. Perhaps the most accepted of these is the idea that evil exists as a contrast to good.

Constructing the Evil Other

The question of what social purpose is served by the existence of evil is relevant to our discussion. In sociological terms, the "in-group" increases its solidarity and cohesion through its identification and active opposition to an "out-group." In fact, an in-group cannot exist without an out-group. The sharper the contrasts between the in-group and the out-group, the more unified the in-group becomes. If an out-group can be perceived as an enemy—as evil—then destroying it becomes justified. This demands, of course, that the "problem," the "enemy," the "evil," always be external—never internal (Stivers 1982, 63). The dilemma in this degree of opposition is that in destroying the out-group, the in-group destroys its own identity. Without the contrast of evil, there is no good.

James Aho's insightful work *This Thing of Darkness: A Sociology of the Enemy* (1994) details the processes of constructing an ideology of hate. The first step is the development of an image of the "other." The enemy (*enema*) is the representation of everything evil and vile about ourselves. The construction of such an enemy then becomes a personal statement as much as an ideological statement. Once the enemy is constructed and the dangers of such a collection of characteristics is noted, the "system" must be purged.

Demonization of the enemy is readily evident in the Christian Identity and British Israelism ideologies, which are the basis of belief in most of the racist hate groups in the U.S.A. today. Racial solidarity is enhanced with the understanding that not only are members of the out-group different, they are evil. What's more, they are not simply evil because they are misled, unformed, or mistaken, but because they were born that way. This becomes a kind of "sociological theodicy." Because one cannot destroy the out-group for fear of also destroying the in-group identity, good cannot destroy evil; it can only accommodate it. White separatism, then, becomes a more realistic institutional goal than genocide. Still, the ideology walks a thin line between tolerating "others" within a separate existence ("Send them back to Africa") and out-group destruction ("Death to all #@!#@!!").

Jeffrey Reiman addressed a similar dilemma in the criminal justice system by explaining that the justice system is not interested in eradicating crime, but in creating a permanent criminal class that is an out-group. Accomplishing this task creates a solidarity among the in-group (upstanding, law-abiding citizens) and intensifies their belief in the rationality of the system. The criminal justice system, in essence, creates solidarity by not only failing to control crime but also by making a show of its failure.

Capitalism

In one sense, it is difficult to completely separate sexism and capitalism. In order for capitalism to be successful, it requires unrestrained competition. This competition requires differentiation—a separation of the deserving and the undeserving. In 1776, when Adam Smith first pub-

lished *The Wealth of Nations*, he advocated competition by constructing
better products that consumers would buy. Unfortunately, it also meant
maximizing profits by minimizing the support of workers (Marx 1975).
This essential ingredient of capitalism occurs through a variety of
means, including a supportive, materialist ideology promoting individualism (Weber 1958/1920).

In a society where individuality is stressed, people take a personal responsibility for their achievements. The American Dream takes on a central importance for those who achieve it because they can claim an
entitlement. Those who have not accumulated the fruits of society may
see themselves as failures. Such self-blame would admit a lack of judgment, intelligence, incentive, or other highly valued characteristics. The
alternative is to blame an unjust system (for example, government), or to
blame another visible but defenseless social group (for example, the
poor), or both (for example, liberals). In such a world, popularly perceived
social problems like crime, poverty, economic recessions, urban decay,
educational failure, drug and alcohol abuse, and violence, among others,
are conveniently blamed on a highly visible lower class of minority people. A central tenet of the American Dream is, after all, that anyone who
wants to "make it" can. Those who cannot compete obstruct the path of
those who are trying desperately to achieve the unattainable American
Dream. They are the albatross around America's collective neck; they
are, by definition, evil.

GOOD AND EVIL: SCRIPTS FOR ACTION

Maintaining a definition of evil requires the construction of social
myths (Ricoeur 1969, 162–63). These myths are created and perpetuated
in a popular culture that provides, not only a generalized ideology, but
specific scripted responses for dealing with good and evil. These myths
are repeated continually in soap operas, hockey games, television shows,
video games, cartoons, and the myriad leisure-time activities in which
Americans engage. These scripts provide social cohesion through shared
experience. The individualist, however, is required to look beyond conventional responses and develop new scripts.

Ideology

Perhaps one of the most well-known scripts for hate groups is *The
Turner Diaries* (Pierce 1980 [1978]): the so-called "bible" of the Patriot
movement (SPLC 1996). Briefly, *The Turner Diaries* outlines the fictional experiences of "patriot" Earl Turner in a future war of the government against the people. The book begins with government agents
confiscating guns from the homes of citizens. Individual rights have been

suspended, and the government (run by Jews and racial minorities) is dictatorial and tyrannical. Turner attempts to resist alone, but he soon stumbles into a widespread "leaderless resistance" movement. Turner becomes the model revolutionary, launching attacks on government buildings, newspaper offices, and minority-owned businesses, rationalizing his actions as the story unfolds. By the end of the novel, Turner is a member of an elite inner circle of revolutionary patriots known as "The Order." As justice prevails, the white revolution takes over the West Coast. Minority people are forced to flee. The remaining United States is a culture with a high density of minority people who are incompetent and easily taken over by an intelligent, hard-working, white army.

In the diary, Turner discusses the rationale and justification for each action. He recounts his own misgivings but always looks at the larger picture of the contribution to "the white race." More than simply a suspenseful (and highly racist) spy thriller, it is a blueprint for action. Each step is presented along with the anticipated response of government and minorities (the enemy). In spite of the fact that this book is available in libraries and (until now) was unavailable in bookstores, more than 200,000 copies have been sold (SPLC 1996). At least one of those copies went to the convicted Oklahoma City Federal Building bomber Timothy McVeigh, who kept a copy with him constantly, memorizing passages. McVeigh, who has been linked to the Elohim City Christian Identity compound, used the rationalizations from *The Turner Diaries* and the instructions on the construction and placement of a bomb made of nitrogen fertilizer and fuel oil to blow up the Oklahoma City Federal Building on 19 April 1995, killing 168 and injuring hundreds more. The rationalization for this type of bombing in *The Turner Diaries* is clear:

But there is no way we can destroy the System without hurting many thousands of innocent people—no way. It is a cancer too deeply rooted in our flesh. And if we don't destroy the System before it destroys us—if we don't cut this cancer out of our living flesh—our whole race will die.

Each day we make decisions and carry out actions which result in the deaths of White persons, many of them innocent of any offense which we consider punishable. We are willing to take the lives of these innocent persons, because a much greater harm will ultimately befall our people if we fail to act now. Our criterion is the ultimate good of our race. (Pierce 1978, 98)

For Pierce's readers and followers, at least two messages are crystal clear: "We are truly the instruments of God in the fulfillment of His Grand Design" (Pierce 1978, 71), and "there is no way to win the struggle in which we are engaged without shedding torrents—veritable rivers—of blood" (Pierce 1978, 79).

Bombs R Us

The highly motivated racist has a wide array of sources for materials. Hate scripts are found in novels, books, monthly newsletters, occasional papers, and the like. If one does not have a knowledge of demolitions, instructions are widely available from many sources. Many resources can be bought in bookstores, by mail order, or on the World Wide Web (see chapter 2 here). Among the more comprehensive and pernicious Web sites was an untitled document that revealed how to make firebombs, napalm, match-head bombs, fuse ignition firebombs, gunpowder, ammonal, thermite reactions, acetone hydrogen explosives, plastic explosives, thermite explosives, TNT, nitroglycerine, chlorine gas, grain elevator explosions, and so on. The implications of the easy availability of such literature is driven home weekly, if not nightly, on local, televised newscasts.

If potential "patriots" are not interested in using bombs, many groups provide manuals on other aspects of warfare. The Militia of Montana, for example, provides such provocative titles as *Improvised Weapons of the American Underground*; *The Advanced Anarchist Arsenal: Recipes for Improvised Incendiaries and Explosives*; *The Ultimate Sniper*; *Black Books: Improvised Munitions*; *Improvised Explosives: How to Make Your Own*; *Vigilante Handbook*; *To Break a Tyrant's Chains: Neo-Guerilla Techniques for Combat*; *Sniper Training and Employment*; *Hand-to-Hand Fighting*; *Counter-intelligence*; *Browning Machinegun Caliber .50 HB*; *M2 Field Manual*; *Special Forces Recon Manual*; and *Grenades and Pyrotechnic Signals*.

This guerilla literature provides rationalizations, procedures, and precise techniques for carrying out a genocidal or separatist war. In dramaturgical terms, it provides both the scripts and props necessary for a particular presentation. For example, what should you do if "the Government" comes to confiscate your weapons? Why should we hate Jews? (or any other minority). What will the "End Times" be like, and how should we prepare for them? How do you join the "resistance"?

Superheroes

American culture encourages each person to be a superhero. The biggest box-office hits are often movies depicting rugged, courageous individuals with a clear notion of the difference between good and evil. Although the core code of bureaucracy is found often in American popular culture (Deegan 1989a), social dramas often depict it as corrupt. Indolent government employees, corrupt cops, and self-interested politicians protect "the system" that they control. If the system is not the problem, it is at least powerless to deal with the evil. It is only through the best efforts of an independent superhero that evil can be conquered and a legitimate bureaucracy installed.

WHO IS EVIL?

Professional Wrestling

Somewhere between the peaks of movie superheroes and children's cartoons lies the valley of professional wrestling. This is a region where the heroes and villains are as transparent as the Coyote and Roadrunner. Good always wins (eventually), and evil is only temporarily dissuaded—never completely destroyed.

Central to these morality plays is the role of the "Ritual Villain," the in-group's nemesis. Villains are divided most conveniently into three major categories: Common Villains, Arrogant Villains, and Global Villains. "Common Villains" break the rules, not out of some sense of honor or commitment, but for the sheer pleasure of it. These thoroughly evil beings include punks, sadists, masked villains, and negative authority figures, all of whom have made the decision to abandon any notion of morality. Although many Common Villains are depicted as mentally retarded or psychotic, they are villains nonetheless. They are guiltless sociopaths uninterested in the "sport" of wrestling and intent upon inflicting pain and terrorizing opponents. "Arrogant Villains" are less "evil," but are nonetheless dangerous because of the "power" they hold. They believe themselves superior to others by virtue of their title, education, money, or other ill-gotten status. As an example, Ted DiBiase (aka "Million Dollar Man") was said to have achieved his wealth through "oil money." King Harley Race and King Haku are both Arrogant Villains crowned by themselves or their managers. Swaggering Nature Boys similarly flaunt their youth and good looks, but they are undeserving because they do not have to "work at" their success (Ball 1990).

Global Villains are international stereotypes based on America's political enemies. The exact list of enemies, of course, changes with the international political atmosphere. Although they espouse ethnic or national allegiance, this is overshadowed by personal avarice and desire for power. Russians espouse communist commitment, but reveal their true capitalist motives. Arabs flaunt their religion, but talk about personal gain. Serious political, economic, or religious ideology is thereby trivialized by the suggestion that their "real motivation" is greed (Ball 1990).

These three types of villains can be analyzed with Deegan's core codes. Common Villains violate the bureaucratically imposed rules to obtain personal gain—often money, prestige, power, or perverse pleasure. Global Villains reflect racial and ethnic concerns, utilizing core code rules similar to sexism. Ethnic types with whom we are not politically aligned become villains, while our political allies become ethnic heroes. Arrogant Villains are associated with class concerns. They are nearly always suspected of achieving their high position outside the normal bureaucratic channels. Having broken the rules, they flaunt their ill-gotten gains by suggesting moral superiority (Ball 1990).

Video Games

While television and "professional" sports are nonparticipatory rituals, a number of other popular cultural activities allow for full participation. These activities are powerful in that they require the destruction of an enemy and active participation to carry out that objective.

A brief tour of local video arcades during the summer of 1995 revealed that around two-thirds of the games were devoted to war or war-like activities in which the objective was the death of the opponent. The remaining games, while competitive in nature (e.g., reinforcing codes of capitalism), were less confrontationally violent (e.g., crashing race cars into a retaining wall instead of crushing an opponent's skull with an ax). We observed the most popular games and confirmed the consistency of our observations with the arcade manager. This is a brief sketch of the four most popular games:

Tekken 2

This is a hand-to-hand fighting game. Players assume a hero's role (e.g., Marshall Law, Paul Phoenix, Lei Wulong, Yoshimitsu) with specific characteristics, like speed or strength, and ethnic stereotypes. The heroes meet in an arena and try to inflict a number of injuries on their enemies using machine gun blow, neutron bomb, jaw breaker, shoulder pop, bone breaker, gut buster, hi-jack backbreaker, death slash, death copter, and so on.

Knights of the Round

This combat game occurs in a "Dungeons and Dragons" setting. Again, there is an array of preconstructed heroes with particular characteristics. Heroes may ascend to higher levels by prevailing over various armor-clad enemies. Heroes are cleancut, physically fit, and straightforward while villains are monstrous beasts with hideous facial features and glowing eyes, often attacking the hero by surrounding him.

Primal Rage

This game depicts a battle between prehistoric beasts. The goal is to kill another dinosaur by biting, clawing, punching, or hitting with the tail. It is interesting to note that a "native" human population observes the battle from a distance. When one of the giant combatants falls, the humans rush out and begin bowing and praying to it. The victorious dinosaur wins the allegiance of the natives.

Cibersled

This is a virtual reality tank game. Participants sit in a seat that jiggles with explosions and listen to the battle through stereo speakers. Players maneuver a tank-like vehicle around an obstacle-filled arena where they compete with computerized enemies.

While the setting of each game varies, the theme remains constant: The player is a "good guy," embodying all the characteristics of heroes, including a willingness to risk injury or death to overcome evil (or for fun). The villain is unreasonable, ugly, vicious, and sly. The solution to each confrontation is the same: kill or be killed. No game is based on negotiation, fairness, or diplomacy. All games define the terms for winning or losing, and the most popular games were often the most violent.

The arcades are somewhat representative of the computer games available for home computers. Although a comprehensive investigation of all available games on home computers and game machines (Sega) would be impossible, a random review of some cases is instructive.

Video Game Packages

The *Defcon 5* (Celery Software, 1993) package contains the following statement:

You are at the controls of America's Strategic Defense Initiative (S.D.I.), [the] "Star Wars" space based missile defense system. Your computer is in command of a network of orbiting visual reconnaissance satellites and an awesome arsenal of sophisticated space based weapons. Using realistic military commands, you control nine separate weapon systems including: Land based chemical lasers, space based free electron lasers, neutron particle beam weapons, electromagnetic launchers, and many more. The fate of the world is in your hands. Will you destroy the missiles in time to save the human race?

Another popular game, *Resurrection, Rise 2* (Aklaim Entertainment) promotes mass violence as the solution to the problem at hand:

It's the age of killing machines, and you're armed for warfare: . . . 18 next generation robots and over 300 devastating moves assure that without annihilation . . . there can be no RESURRECTION!

Several points are noteworthy. The first game promotes a current controversial weapons system. Although the tactics and elements of the system are inaccurate, the name is provocatively alluring to children. In both cases, there is no specific enemy. The point is not to use force as a last resort to protect home, family, and country; simply use it for the "fun" of destroying an enemy—any enemy. Violence, mass violence, is the solution to destroying evil.

Of course software stores also provide many non–war-related games. These include those categorized as "action-adventure," often "Dungeons and Dragons" scenarios in which slaying a dragon or an evil enemy is part of the game. Nor are games for small children exempt. *Gearheads* (Philips Media) advertises, "a furious war of wind-up toys."

Cyber-Hate: What a Tangled Web We Weave

It is only a small step from popular cultural activities that reinforce ideologies of hate to hate becoming a popular cultural activity in itself. With the development of the "Information Super-Highway," we complete that circle. The Southern Poverty Law Center (SPLC 1996, 18) estimated that "By January 1996, there were at least 50 internet newsgroups and more than 70 World Wide Web pages catering to antigovernment extremists, survivalists, Identity followers, white supremacists, militiamen and would-be terrorists." My own research at roughly the same time revealed approximately 120 World Wide Web pages devoted to different hate groups, with many dozens more indirectly linked.

William Pierce (Head of the National Alliance and author of *The Turner Diaries*) reports that when his Web site opened in October of 1995, more than 500 people accessed it daily. Recently that number climbed to an average of 1,764 users daily. Pierce reports that the Web is

a more effective medium for us than most, because the persons who see our message via this medium are persons of somewhat higher quality, in terms of intelligence and attainment, than the average for the population.

Our message can be expected to have more of an impact on someone who wants to see it and looks for it on the Internet than on some Joe Sixpack who finds an unrequested leaflet in his screen door or under his windshield wiper. (SPLC 1996)

The significance of these pages is the ability to communicate across great distance—even internationally. With limited communication in the pre-cyber days, individual racists were separated by distance, the slowness of mail, and the difficulty of physical travel. Communication was generally through organizational publications, letters to acquaintances, or word of mouth in specific geographical areas. Consequently, isolated individual racists may have received little local reinforcement for their views. With hate groups now utilizing computer technology, there are dozens of different Web pages and hundreds of "chat groups" devoted to racism. One can now receive not only instant reinforcement of racist beliefs, but also absorb new ideas, create new rationalizations, and participate in more meetings and campaigns.

The new ability of hate groups to share ideologies has resulted in a uniform jargon and worldview across groups. "Christian Identity," for example, now forms the central belief system for formerly diverse hate groups like the Ku Klux Klan, Nazis, militias, and skinheads (see chapter 2). The core ideology is shared by various groups, although the specific order of elements may vary. A person may be a Klan Christian with a gun, or a Christian militia member who believes that Jews are the "spawn of Satan," or a Patriot who believes that minorities are responsible for the problems of the U.S.A. and, therefore, supports the ideology of Christian Identity. As communication increases, we find the Arkansas Ku Klux Klan talking about ZOG (a militia term) and the "Adamic race" (a Christian Identity term). Just as commonly, Patriots (Christian Posse Comitatus 1996) discuss white supremacy or separatism and Christianity (a Christian Identity term).

JUSTIFYING VIOLENCE

We live in an era when the eradication of social problems is suggested by declaring "war" on them. Perhaps the first major (although unsuccessful) social fight was Lyndon Johnson's "War on Poverty." Poverty was so disturbing that we declared it an enemy and demonized it. This allowed us to use violence (although largely rhetorical) to end it. More recently, we witnessed the "war on drunk drivers" and the "war on drugs." Although the process is the same, we now have a literal license to violently eradicate evil. With more police, courts, and prisons, we can identify and punish more "criminals." We can invade other countries and kill their citizens in a "holy" quest to destroy drug evil. Perhaps the ultimate irony is our present concern over violence: We are now ready to declare "war" on violence.

The striking similarity in the popular cultural activities discussed above is that they all script action for the violent destruction of evil. The action is not directed toward negotiating with an enemy nor bargaining with a competitor, but toward resolutely crushing evil. Although the circumstances differ, the themes remain remarkably similar.

HATE, EVIL AND THE AMERICAN DREAM

There is little question of the growing disaffection of the American public with elements of government and business. Both the "left" and the "right" might agree that particular problems are symptoms of breakdowns in some aspect of American society—rising violent crime, high divorce rates, drug and alcohol addiction, governmental overregulation, high taxes, the pervasive influence of big business, and so on. The dispute is generally not the fact that problems exist; it is with their causes and how to deal with them.

If we create a popular culture that values rugged individualism, unreasoning hatred, divisiveness, materialism, and violence, is it any wonder that we also create individuals who utilize these scripted "solutions" to social problems? Those who propose censorship and increased social control do not recognize the depth of the problem. We could remove violence from television and movies, shut down the arcades, and ban Nazis from the Internet. But while these are undoubtedly corrupting influences, they reflect much larger social values that we encourage. Covering the mirror is not the solution. Little is accomplished by "declaring war" on such problems as long as the ideology that promotes differentiation, hate, and materialism remains attractive.

NOTE

1. I am indebted to my student research assistant, Brian Thorbjornsen, Rev. Dr. Raleigh Peterson who provided me with some lessons on good and evil, Leland Sarmont and Jeanne Faulkner who assisted with acquisition of some key resources, Doug Martineau in the University of Wisconsin-Superior mail room, and the students in my spring 1996 "Hate Groups Seminar."

III

Sexism as a Core Code in American Ritual

4

The Case of Amateur Stripping: Sex Codes and Egalitarianism in a Heterosocial Setting

Thomas C. Calhoun, Rhonda Fisher, and Julie Ann Harms Cannon[1]

Egalitarianism is the idealized pattern of authority in gendered relationships in the United States. Attempts at gender equality include the first and second waves of the women's movement, and most recently, affirmative action. Despite these structural attempts at gender equality, a gross discrepancy exists between the ideal of egalitarianism and reality. Complete egalitarianism can only be realized when men and women have equal and attainable resource opportunities. The resulting dissonance is often alleviated through even greater fabrication, which becomes very creative and well disguised.

Professional stripping, an occupation that has traditionally been done by women for men, serves as a glaring example of overt sexism in this society. In a move toward pseudo-egalitarianism, women have only recently been allowed access to the world of commercialized sex-related entertainment vis-à-vis the male strip show. Since the mid- to late-1970s, more bars and nightclubs have begun to feature male strippers, and researchers have begun to explore the differences (Dressel and Peterson 1982a, 1982b; Peterson and Dressel 1982; Margolis and Arnold 1993).

The primary differences between male and female professional stripping environments can be found in the setting and in the audience. David Peterson and Paula Dressel (1982) noted that male strip clubs propagate the notion of the "egalitarian motif": the opportunity to be like men in terms of aggressive sexual behavior representing a form of equal rights for women.

Maxine L. Margolis and Marigene Arnold (1993) challenge the notion of egalitarianism in a comparison of male strip shows and the more traditional ones that feature female dancers. They hypothesize that, if the male strip show is a true inversion of traditional gender hierarchy, then "it should be a mirror image of the female strip show with only the sex of the performers and the audience reversed" (p. 335). Margolis and Arnold detail the following factors about male strippers, which demonstrate that the role reversal is illusory: Male dancers are depicted as sexual aggressors; they interact only as performers and not as wait staff; their job is one that evokes interest because of its novelty; they are referred to as "artistic" and "sexy" versus a "whore" or a "slut"; and their financial compensation is higher.

If an environment existed in which both male and female stripping occurred, with all things being "equal," would true egalitarianism exist? The amateur stripping competition provides an excellent opportunity to explore the "egalitarian motif" and do what other researchers have not been able to do: explore the phenomena of male and female stripping, controlling for setting and the audience. We define "amateurs" as those individuals who engage in stripping primarily during contests, but who do not see stripping as a full- or part-time occupation. Further, we argue that if true egalitarianism exists, there should be no major differences between male and female performances or audience-performer interactions.

Our objective in this chapter is to document the unique interaction rituals of the amateur strip bar in a heterosocial setting using the theoretical perspectives of Erving Goffman (1974) and Mary Jo Deegan (1989a). Additionally, we will present observations (also termed "strips of activity" by Goffman 1974) and discuss amateur stripping and audience interaction at a popular midwestern college bar.[2]

LITERATURE REVIEW

Charles McCaghy and James Skipper (1969; Skipper and McCaghy 1970; McCaghy and Skipper 1972), pioneers in the field of stripping research, focused on the external motivations, sexual orientation, and social interactions of female strippers. Since that original research, social scientists have begun to explore the motivational factors and identity maintenance of primarily female strippers. Only two scientific studies to our knowledge have spotlighted males who engage in stripping as an occupation (Dressel and Peterson 1982a, 1982b; Peterson and Dressel 1982; Margolis and Arnold 1993). In addition, previous research has focused exclusively on the work done by professional strippers. There is currently, to our knowledge, no published empirical research on amateur stripping or the heterosocial, seemingly egalitarian, setting in which it takes place.

In the following sections, we will discuss the major areas of interest on stripping research: motivations (internal versus external), interaction patterns and occupational norms, and, finally, identity work and development.

Motivations

Consistently, researchers pointed to the external rewards of stripping. Economic gain appeared to be the primary motivation for both female and male strippers (Skipper and McCaghy 1970; Carey, Peterson and Sharpe 1974; Peterson and Dressel 1982; Dressel and Peterson 1982b; Ronai and Ellis 1989; Reid, Epstein and Benson 1994a, 1994b). According to Skipper and McCaghy (1970), a financial crisis preceded the first paid stripping incident and was characteristic for female strippers. Women felt forced to strip in order to meet some financial need. In addition, stripping was likely to be the primary source of income for the female stripper.

Male strippers, on the other hand, were more likely to engage in stripping as purely a tax-free, extra-occupational venture. However, "a major difference which exists between male and female stripping is that women apparently do not become strippers for sexual outlet" (Dressel and Peterson 1982b, 394). Hence, male strippers often engage in stripping as a source of sexual pleasure or gratification. Other motivations for male strippers include gifts and favors, excitement inherent in entertainment work, ready means of meeting women, and utilizing stripping as an entrée into another entertainment career (Dressel and Peterson 1982b).

Sexual Orientation

Because of the sexual nature of stripping as an occupation, researchers have been quick to address the sexual orientation of the participants (McCaghy and Skipper 1969; Carey, Peterson and Sharpe 1974; Peterson and Dressel 1982; Dressel and Peterson 1982a, 1982b; Reid, Epstein and Benson 1994b). This focus has been especially prevalent in, but not limited to, research on female strippers. It is important to note that while the literature on female strippers focuses on "lesbianism" or homosexuality between performers (McCaghy and Skipper 1969; Carey, Peterson and Sharpe 1974; Reid, Epstein and Benson 1994a, 1994b), the literature on male strippers overemphasizes the heterosexual function of the club setting and not the sexual orientation of the performer or sexual activity between performers (Peterson and Dressel 1982; Dressel and Peterson 1982a, 1982b).

In their in-depth interviews of thirty-five female strippers, McCaghy and Skipper (1969) identified homosexuality as an important aspect of the stripping occupation. Their focus was on structural factors rather than individual predispositions that might lead to homosexual behavior, and they viewed the occupation of stripping as having similar characteristics to that of a "total institution" (that is, a prison setting, Goffman 1961). For female strippers, homosexuality, or lesbianism, had several reasons: the result of situational factors resulting from structural aspects of the occupation, including isolation (strippers are frequently "on the road"); unsatisfactory relationships with males (within and outside of the occupation); and, finally, work within an occupational structure that seemingly allows a wide range of sexual behavior (McCaghy and Skipper 1969).

Interaction Patterns and Occupational Norms

Research on stripping has focused also on interaction patterns among strippers, customers, managers, bouncers, and announcers, as well as on occupational norms (McCaghy and Skipper 1969; Skipper and McCaghy 1970; Carey, Peterson and Sharpe 1974; Peterson and Dressel 1982; Dressel and Peterson 1982b; Peretti and O'Connor 1989; Ronai and Ellis 1989). The types of settings and methods of entertainment determined the interaction strategies and occupational norms of the strippers.

The "homosocial setting" (Peterson and Dressel 1982), which is typically and frequently mandatory in male strip clubs, is also typical of bars that feature female strippers, and provides a supportive environment for the expression of socially constructed traditional and nontraditional gender roles. For example, in the female stripping environment, the audience members (primarily men) are encouraged to play out traditionally masculine gender roles, while in the male stripping environment, the audience members (primarily female) are encouraged to transcend traditionally female gender roles and take on sexually assertive behavior typically associated with the male gender role (Peterson and Dressel 1982).

Further, the confirmation of gender roles (traditional or nontraditional) is demonstrated through the use of exaggerated "heterosexual imagery" (Peterson and Dressel 1982). Through the use of props and costumes (firefighter, construction worker, Tarzan, Superman, and so on) male strippers seek to magnify and personalize heterosexuality. This heterosexual imagery is a crucial element of the homosocial setting (Peterson and Dressel 1982).

Treatment of interaction strategies have dealt primarily with customer–stripper interactions. The purpose of this interaction was to maximize financial gain for the strippers. Financial gain is increased by a strategy labeled "counterfeiting of intimacy" (Enck and Preston 1988; Boles and Garbin 1974), in which the strippers pretend to actually care about or desire a relationship with the customer in order to obtain larger financial reward. Strippers typically manipulated their customers by feigning personal interest.

For both male and female strippers, spatial intimacy or close proximity to the customer tends to be the most lucrative form of interaction. Variations of table dancing appeared to be the most efficient breakdown of social distance between the customer and the strippers (Peterson and Dressel 1982; Boles and Garbin 1974; Ronai and Ellis 1989). However, it should be noted that some strippers are actually interested in maintaining relationships with customers that go beyond the stripping situation (Ronai and Ellis 1989; Dressel and Peterson 1982a, 1982b; Peterson and Dressel 1982). These relationships are usually sexual in nature and frequently involve prostitution (Baron 1989).

Identity

In terms of identity, the current focus of stripping research is on the formation and maintenance of a positive identity for strippers (Reid, Epstein, and Benson 1994a, 1994b; Ronai and Ellis 1989; Peretti and O'Connor 1989; Dressel and Peterson 1982). However, the identity-maintenance strategies differ for males and females. While male strippers endeavor to justify their stripping behavior, female strippers attempt to reduce the stigma surrounding the occupation (Mullen 1985; Thompson and Harred 1992). Thomas Calhoun (1992) observed a similar pattern in his study of young male prostitutes. This seems quite logical based on notions of traditional or "appropriate" gender role behavior: It seems likely that stripping, as an occupation, holds a much greater negative social stigma for female strippers than for male strippers.

In their study of 41 female strippers, Scott A. Reid, Jonathon A. Epstein, and D. E. Benson (1994a, 1994b) found that the exotic identity is not central to the female stripper's self-concept. Further, most of the strippers in their study did not perceive the characteristics of their deviant occupations as reflective of their personal values. Again, the strippers work for the money and are able to separate their personal identities from their occupations. They use this occupation for its short-term benefits to enhance other areas of their lives that are more central to their self-concepts or identities (students or mothers).

To maintain distance from the stripping role, male and female strippers use various strategies to avoid "identity contamination" (Reid, Epstein and Benson 1994a, 1994b). Male strippers maintain that their occupational choice serves the needs of newly "liberated" women. Justification strategies developed by male strippers include the following: Stripping provides liberated women with a social outlet; male stripping provides women with an environment in which they can be sexually assertive; stripping can be seen as a sexual outlet for women who would otherwise not have partners; and, finally, stripping is a unique form of commercial entertainment (Dressel and Peterson 1982b). In addition to providing a sexual outlet and commercial entertainment, women's justifications also include an instructional aspect. Strippers are often approached by women seeking sexual advice (Boles and Garbin 1974).

Stripping research to date has focused exclusively on professional strippers in a homosocial setting. Amateur stripping provides a unique opportunity to explore not only those individuals who strip for prize money and tips, but it also provides insight into a heterosocial environment where the phenomena of socially constructed egalitarianism can be examined. Although foundational, literature on male and female professional stripping is limited in interpreting the amateur stripping ritual. Because amateur stripping takes place in a heterosocial rather than a homosocial setting, alternative models must be developed to fully explain this phenomenon.

THEORETICAL FOUNDATION

The development of the theoretical framework to analyze the amateur stripping ritual is grounded in Goffman's (1974) work on "framing" and its extension by Deegan's (1989a) work on the "core codes" of American rituals. Although Deegan's work entitled, "The Meet/Meat Market Ritual," does not specifically address the stripping ritual, key elements of the singles bar scene can be applied to amateur stripping.

Goffman (1959) defends the view that the physical world exists and has a primary reality. Situations have organization, a set of contingencies, and constraints that may enter into the definition of the situation but that are not merely created by the defining process. Situations are multidimensional and layered. Not only does each person have his or her own appraisal of the situation, but each person can be in several complex layers of situational definitions at the same time. Goffman's purpose was to show that everyday life is not simple and that people deal with its complexity as a matter of ordinary common sense (Goffman 1974). Goffman's frames are designed to avoid complete relativism and yet call to mind the existence of multiple realities. Frames organize levels of meaning and involvement.

"Core Codes" and Alienation

Goffman concludes:

> that everyday experience is characterized by the ever present possibility that interactions are deceptive, that is, organized by making reference to fabricated frames. This chronic condition generates alienated experience because actors are never sure if they are being duped. (Deegan 1989a, 13)

Deegan (1989a) argues that rituals have the potential to liberate individuals from their mundane existences—this would be a positive function of rituals (Turner 1982). Rituals have the potential to "free" us from the confines of the everyday world. However, Deegan (1989a) and Goffman (1974) primarily focus on the negative aspects of American rituals, with Deegan's work extending Goffman's in several important ways.[3] Although Deegan extends Goffman's work on interpersonal interaction to the macrosocial level, both acknowledge the potentially alienating effect of rituals in Western culture.

Although Goffman's work on strips, frames, and interaction rituals is especially valuable to the study of stripping behavior, his analysis lacks the sophistication to investigate the structural components of the stripping phenomenon. Stripping is much more than the face-to-face interactions of the participants. Amateur stripping, we contend, occurs within existing social structures that perpetuate social inequality. For this reason, it is imperative that we turn to the "core codes" that regulate gendered "fun" in this culture (see chapter 1). Deegan's (1989a) analysis of gender inequality in American rituals is especially useful at this point: She uses the concept of "core codes" to distinguish the characteristics of American rituals, including interaction rituals, that perpetuate existing social inequalities. Deegan notes specifically that rules that produce and reproduce sexism may be labeled "sex codes." She contends that it is the rules of the "sex code" in American society that foster the alienation of individuals (see chapter 1).

The purpose of this chapter is to analyze the ritual of amateur stripping through the lens of Deegan's core codes. Specifically, we examine the ways in which the "egalitarian motif" operates as a "sex code" within a heterosocial setting. We focus primarily on the oppressive nature of the "sex code" and on the creation of social inequality of women who participate in the amateur stripping ritual. In addition, we utilize a concept designated "beauty code," an extension of the "sex code." The "beauty code" regulates the stripping ritual, and meeting or not meeting the standards of the "beauty code" determines whether or not individuals win or lose the competition.

METHODS

Subjects and Setting

The subjects of our research are the contest participants (amateur strippers), audience members, announcers, disc jockeys, and security staff who participate in an amateur stripping contest at a popular college bar in a Midwestern city. The contest is open to men and women and occurs once a week, on Thursday, the most popular "night out." The only fee is the $2 cover charge that everyone pays upon entry. In each of the two contests—one for men, one for women—participants compete for one of three available prizes: first place, $100; second place, $50; and third place, $25.

The contest takes place in a very dimly lit bar atmosphere and is virtually the same each week. The dance floor is at center stage, with tables and chairs surrounding the floor. There is also a second level to the bar, where audience members can view the competition from above the dance floor—almost like a balcony area at a theater. Alcoholic beverages and pool tables are available to customers on both levels of the bar. During our four-month investigation, we observed on the average five male and five female participants in the weekly dance contest. Some nights the number of participants in each contest was as high as eleven. However, at no event did the number of participants fall below three in each contest. In each contest, the majority of participants were caucasian; however, on various occasions, some were African-American, some, Hispanic Americans, and a few, Asian Americans. The participants appeared to be approximately 21 to 25 years of age.

Data Collection and Techniques

Consistent with previous stripping research, we employ qualitative research methods. Ethnographic or qualitative methods solve many dilemmas encountered when doing research with individuals engaging in stigmatized behavior (Anderson and Calhoun 1992). The data for this project was obtained through our participation and observations as audience members at a local amateur stripping competition. We conceptualized this project as a case study of a weekly, local, "egalitarian" amateur stripping contest.

We recorded data by direct observation and note-taking during the contest. We made observations from several locations in the bar in order to examine participants' behavior from different vantage points. We wrote our notes and observations after each competition and analyzed our data at a later date. Extensive note-taking during the competition, although possible, was not a feasible research strategy. In order to become a part of the setting, we had to downplay our roles as researchers. However, as audience members inquired about our presence and note-taking, we told them the purpose of our project. This yielded several important, unsolicited responses from audience members that proved to be valuable.

FINDINGS

Egalitarianism and the Heterosocial Setting

Constructing the Subtle "Egalitarian Motif"

The bar that sponsors the amateur strip night or contest will be referred to as Kato's (all names used in this study are pseudonyms). Amateur stripping appears to be a major source of entertainment for college-aged students, and it is held on Thursday, the "prime" partying night in this large Midwestern college town.

Amateur strip night provides the business entrepreneur with a new consumer market for commercialized sexual entertainment. As a capitalistic endeavor, amateur strip night generates income for the bar's employees and especially the owners. The expenditures for the evening involve the overhead of the facility, prize money ($350 total), salaries for the announcer, the security staff, the disc jockey, the bartenders, and the wait staff, who work primarily for tips.

At Kato's, the main sources of revenue are the $2 cover charge and the sale of alcoholic beverages, which can be purchased at three fixed locations or from wait staff at the tables. In order to maximize the sale of alcohol, Kato's has two main bars (upstairs and downstairs), a mini-bar immediately inside the door, and wait staff (only women) who take orders from the tables. In addition, approximately 45 minutes before the contest begins, the announcer offers "shots" or drinks for $1.50 (Tequila Sunrise, Rum and Coke, Cocksucker, and so on). We speculate that alcohol is available to "loosen up" the audience members, by either inducing them to strip later in the evening or encouraging their friends to do so.

Most patrons arrive at Kato's at least an hour early because of the limited seating. While they wait, individuals may dance alone, in groups of two or three, or in a very large group dance called the "Electric Slide," which can be danced to a variety of songs. Men and women who come to Kato's for the express purpose of stripping rarely give a preview by dancing prior to the competition.

The audience members appear to be equally gender balanced and number from 125–150 on a typical night. Primarily college-aged, audience members are proportionately racially/ethnically diverse for this Midwestern city, with a university population of 25,000. For the men's competition—the first event of the evening—women line the dance floors. As soon as the competition is over, there is a very aggressive readjustment of space and atmosphere as men take over the inside perimeter of the dance floor to view the women who will participate in the upcoming contest.

When a performance is considered exceptional by the audience, members respond in several ways. As a group, there is a general rowdiness and chanting of "Take that shit off." Individually, members may give the stripper a ritual monetary offering for their momentary and exclusive attention. The presentation and acceptance of the "tip" can also be done in a variety of ways. Occasionally, women may place the bill between their breasts, step onto the dance floor, and begin to dance, expecting the male stripper to reciprocate. Most often however, women or men lay flat on the floor with the bill in their teeth, in the waistband of their jeans, their zipper, or between their knees.

We speculate that the subtlety of the fabricated "egalitarian motif" (Peterson and Dressel 1982) in a heterosocial setting provides patrons with the sense that they are at a "typical" night club.[4] Thus, Kato's is not seen as a seedy men's stripper bar or an all women's night club where the "egalitarian motif" is an overt construction. At Kato's, the environment is "supportive" and "family"-oriented, thus creating the sense that men and women are equally important. However, unlike the overt "egalitarian motif," the subtle "egalitarian motif" does not encourage strippers to transcend traditional gender roles; instead, it perpetuates them. Thus, the nature of the competition is neither liberating nor playful, as Turner (1982) would suggest; it is oppressive in the sense that "sex codes" are maintained and thrive, as Deegan (1989a) contends.

Key Performers and the Competition: The Roles of the Announcer, Disc Jockey, Security Staff, and the Audience

At approximately 10:30 p.m., the disc jockey plays the classic stripper song, "The Stripper," to signal the beginning of the evening's main event. To begin "Amateur Strip Night," the announcer appears and attempts to further build excitement and enthusiasm by calling male strippers over to the disc jockey's booth. Next, he explains the formal rules of the competition, which are fairly simple in that participants (1) must not expose buttocks or genitalia (strippers cannot be nude or wear underwear that is too revealing such as G-strings); (2) cannot touch audience members; and (3) they have three minutes to perform their routine. The formal rules of the contest are easily recognized, as violations are immediately dealt with by the five security staff strategically placed around the dance floor or by the announcer. Participants who violate the rules of the competition or who do not finish their "striptease" are disqualified from the competition.

The announcer at Kato's is a college-aged, caucasian male who dresses casually to fit in with the clientele. The announcer's role is crucial in maintaining the bar's atmosphere and soliciting participants for the contest. Because the audience members know why they are at Kato's and generally know what is expected of them, the announcer's job is much easier. He simply passes the time waiting for audience members to come forward while "The Stripper" song blares in the background. Competitors choose their own music after a brief consultation with the disc jockey and have approximately three minutes to execute the most lucrative and seductive performance, in terms of tips and the ultimate—prize money.

The announcer also proclaims that various rituals are underway. For example, when several audience members rush out and lie down on the floor with their tips exposed, the announcer declares, "It's buffet time!" He also awards the monetary prizes based on his perception of which strippers receive the most verbal response. During our observation period, his decisions were never challenged by the audience, nor did he use sophisticated machinery to measure decibel levels.

The disc jockey at Kato's, a caucasian, college-aged male, has several roles during amateur strip night. His top priority is to keep the music playing so the customers can dance before and after the competition. He also announces drink specials. During the competition, he consults each performer to select or recommend music for his or her routine. Often the performers do not have a song in mind, and the disc jockey suggests a popular song for them to use.

The bouncers/security guards are easily identifiable by their black T-shirts or "tanks" labeled "SECURITY." They appear to be college-aged men with much larger than average physiques. (There are no female bouncers/security guards.) Part of their job, aside from crowd control, is to ensure that the strippers do not touch the audience members. To do so, bouncers often get on the floor in a stance similar to that of a wrestling referee before the "takedown" and verbally reprimand the stripper or tipper for any indiscretions. Since strippers simulate the sex act as well as "oral sex," touching does occur, but disqualification for this type of rule-breaking was never witnessed by the researchers—bouncers often look the other way.

The bouncers also have another function. Occasionally, in an evening without sufficient excitement, enthusiasm, or lack of willing participants, audience members or the announcer may ask the bouncers to strip. Because the bouncers we saw wore ornate underwear, we assumed that bouncers had to be ready to participate in the contest without prior notice.

The men's competition has a dependable opener—The Sandman (pseudonym)—who readily agrees to be the first stripper of the evening.

The following announcement is typical: "OK, do you want to see naked guys? We have one for you. You want him, you need him, you dream about him at night . . . The Sandman!" The crowd waits for him expecting some small variation on his usual jean shorts and boots with chains. The Sandman never actually strips down to his underwear, although he has worn a G-string on the outside of his shorts.

The women, who have no reliable opener, are sometimes reluctant to strip. They are then offered prizes from the announcer (e.g., T-shirts and CDs) and cash from the crowd. Although the men's competition begins first, the women's competition is the main event, thus illustrating the "egalitarian motif." Not surprisingly, the men's competition, given the role of The Sandman, begins quicker and without much coaxing or coercion from the announcer. To maintain traditional gender roles, it is important for the women to exhibit "coy sexuality" (Risman 1987). Women are expected to act "provocatively but within a limit of not being openly available" (Deegan 1989a).

We argue that this "chivalry charade" is intended to represent a true inversion of the traditional gender hierarchy with men and women both getting equal time and stripping down to "equal" underwear. However, viewing the contest through the "sex code," the "egalitarian motif" becomes oppressive and a co-optation of the women's liberation movement. The formal rules epitomize the "egalitarian motif," in that stripping down to "equal" underwear is a fabrication of identical titillation.

Each contest is judged separately, but in a similar manner. After each stripper performs, he or she is "corralled" in an area roped off from the audience and from other potential performers. This area is enthusiastically protected by the security guards or bouncers. The participants remain in this area until all of the men or women have performed, and then they are asked to return to the dance floor for the last "roundup" to secure the prize money. Participants who have put their clothing on return to the floor to do a shortened version of their original performance. After another three minutes of dancing, the announcer asks the strippers to line up in a straight line. Participants jockey for position, allowing the audience a final look before voting for the winner.

Beginning with the first participant, the announcer asks the audience members to cheer for the first contestant, and so on. The winner is chosen subjectively by the announcer based on the performance that receives the highest decibel response, in his opinion. In evaluating the male competition for example, the announcer asks, "Okay, ladies what do you think of The Sandman?" The audience, acknowledging the importance and regularity of The Sandman's role, responds with a smattering of applause. The winning competitors are evaluated by hooting, whistling, and yelling.

Amateur Stripping and the "Beauty Codes"

Beauty Regulations

The "beauty codes" at Kato's are extremely rigid and are framed within the "sex codes." These were derived by observing naturally occurring evaluations and violations of the codes. The "beauty codes" operate at an informal level—but, nevertheless, orchestrate the evening. Participants have eliminated most body hair (chest and pubic hair for men; pubic hair for women) and muscle tone is a highly desirable trait. Excessive muscularity is tolerated, and even desired for male participants, with a smaller waist and "tight buns" also necessary but not sufficient.

The "beauty code" for women is apparently narrower and does not include certain extremes (excessive muscularity). Female participants who receive the most tips have bodies consistent with the "Playboyesque" model of beauty—small waist, hips, and thighs and relatively large breasts. Full-figured or voluptuous women are consistently chosen as winners, although flexibility, tight buttocks, a penchant for bending over and pushing the breasts into close proximity of the male audience members are also rewarded. Women with sagging or small breasts, described by male audience members as "just a bleep on the boob scan," overcompensate by dancing more seductively and enthusiastically than women with large- or average-sized breasts.

Silicone implants in female participants bring about paradoxical evaluations. Jenny, one of the "regulars" who is consistently a contest winner, is excessively thin, making her breast augmentation more obvious. Male audience members, who engage in armchair analysis as breast "connoisseurs," evaluate her more stringently, and her surgical augmentation is viewed as an "enthusiastic" endeavor by Jenny to manipulate the "sport." However, female audience members shout "boob job," and act as if the augmented contestant has in some way "cheated" and should be disqualified.

Regular Performers and "Beauty Code" Violations

The Sandman has been a regular in the competition and, in fact, placed on three occasions at the outset of "Amateur Strip Night" at Kato's and once during our observation period. The Sandman blatantly violates the stripper "beauty codes" with his thick glasses, protruding stomach, and lack of muscle definition; yet The Sandman has a very specific role in the competition. The audience feels confident that the competition can only get better from here on. The announcer's most recent comment, "That's not something you see everyday. Thank God," illustrates this point.

Why The Sandman returns on a weekly basis, knowing that he most likely will not win the competition, is unknown, although part of his weekly performance includes a "Damn!" after he discovers that he has not been chosen—again. He usually only receives a single dollar in tips, although women sometimes throw pennies or napkins onto the floor. His dancing style and song selection are inappropriate for Kato's and he is oblivious to the "beauty codes" and appears to perform for his own enjoyment.

An extreme example illustrating the most basic "beauty code" occurred during an evening's competition in the men's division. A white male, approximately 35 years of age calling himself "Milwaukee Mel," jumped out onto the floor. He appeared to have thinning hair, a "beer gut," as well as lifetime neglect of the "six-month dental checkup." The audience responded with their usual low-level "booing" until a shocking discovery was made: the participant was missing part of his right arm (from above the elbow). The audience, unsure of how to respond, seemed momentarily transfixed.

In a setting where beauty is evaluated openly and seemingly without inhibition, politeness remains an audience norm for those performers with a physical impairment. Mel had obviously violated the very basic "beauty code" of the contest: Participants must have no visible anomalies unless they involve abnormally large breasts or genitalia. Mel was eventually disqualified when he began to reveal his buttocks and was removed by the security staff. The audience seemed visibly relieved as they realized that they would not have to rank Mel in the "roundup" and wrestle uncomfortably with politeness norms in a setting where otherwise there are few.

Women and men must adhere to the basic "beauty codes," but, again, women must also uphold the norm of "coy sexuality" (Risman 1987). Women must appear unprepared to dance because props such as studded underwear, gloves, garters, bustiers, patent leather high-heeled boots, and so on, allude to promiscuity and destroy the illusion of the "virginal stripper."

DISCUSSION AND CONCLUSIONS

The amateur stripping ritual is yet another example, although more subtle, of how the male-dominated society perpetuates the "egalitarian motif." The attempt to normalize the imbalance of stripping for men and women is fabricated since the exposure of the male torso is not viewed as titillating by society at large. Further, the practice is subject to local obscenity laws, which support this reversal, thus demonstrating the institutionalization of the sex code.

While it may be true that male stripping is a reversal in that women have the opportunity to objectify and ogle men's bodies, men's status is not degraded through participation. Their performance is viewed with curiosity and as artistic while women's morals are questioned. In the language overheard at Kato's, the term "stud" is designated solely for men who win the contest, and there is no such positive counterpart for women. Conversely, a term for a male "slut" is never used because stripping is not equated with male morality.

Our findings indicate that egalitarianism at Kato's is a fabrication because the women's contest is really the main event. Under the guise of the "egalitarian motif," Kato's has devised a lucrative scheme whereby young women strip on a weekly basis—most without compensation. Although the contest is portrayed as a liberating experience for men and women, the contest appears to be more "fun" for men and "alienating" or oppressive for women. We argue that the "egalitarian motif" is very carefully constructed, with the male contest legitimizing the female one, perpetuating the status quo sex code while the capitalist code is reinforced by male owners who manipulate women for profit.

Although this case study has provided us with invaluable insights into the amateur stripping ritual occurring within a heterosocial context, future research should investigate how the participants view themselves and how they believe others perceive them. Specifically, does motivation to participate in the activity vary by gender? Further, do women who participate in this activity define it as oppressive, and if so, how do they justify their participation? Finally, do stigma containment strategies operate differentially for men and women in a heterosocial setting? This new wave of amateur stripping research must be carried out through personal interviews.

NOTES

1. We, the authors, list ourselves alphabetically. Each of our contributions to this article is very different yet equally important. We would also like to thank Leon Anderson, Mary Jo Deegan, and Wayne Osgood for comments on an earlier draft of this chapter. Their insights have been invaluable to our work.

2. Goffman employs the use of the term "strip" to refer to "any raw batch of occurrence that one wants to draw attention to as a starting point for analysis" (1974, 10). He refers to "strips of activity" and "strips of experience" as arbitrary slices or cuts from events. Analyses focus on the operations of core codes within society, which deceptively re-create the deeply embedded gender hierarchy.

3. Although Deegan (1989a) focuses primarily on negative aspects of rituals in American culture, she demonstrates, as does Turner (1982b), that rituals can also have a liberating effect when oppressive "core codes" are not in operation.

4. The term "fabrication" as used by Goffman (1974, 83) refers to "the intentional effort of one or more individuals to manage activity so that a party of one or more others will be induced to have a false belief about what it is that is going on."

5

There She Is: The Miss America Pageant as an American Ritual Drama

Lisa K. Nielsen

The Miss America Pageant[1] is a uniquely American icon, and the subject of much public speculation—at least once a year when the contest is held—since 1921. The public discourse about the program's effects on women in our society has been heated for years, even prior to the advent of the publicly prominent feminist movement of the 1960s. Those opposed to the program declare it to be exploitative, a flagrant abuse of who and what women are, and they assert that it trivializes and demeans the female experience. Its advocates heavily emphasize that the Miss America organization is the largest scholarship program for women in the world; it avidly promotes its benefits to the participants as an excellent opportunity for personal development and self-actualization, and to the pageant's community, as a worthy philanthropic effort on the local, state, or national level.

Mary Jo Deegan's *American Ritual Dramas: Social Rules and Cultural Meanings* (1989a) provided a well-defined design to examine data, share impressions, and express my views. Data was derived from documented information such as texts, articles, and interviews; and through my personal experiences as a former Miss America Scholarship Pageant Program contestant and local pageant director. First, this chapter explores the general factors that qualify the Miss America Scholarship Pageant Program (herafter referred to as the Miss America Pageant) as an American ritual drama. Second, the Miss America program is analyzed more specifically as both a participatory and a media-constructed ritual. Third, I illustrate how the program integrates itself into American society at large. And, finally, I conclude with the potential contributions/ramifications the program may hold for women in the future.

THE MISS AMERICA PAGEANT AS AN AMERICAN RITUAL DRAMA

Deegan employs a critical dramaturgical perspective that explains human action as a product of rules and "scripts" for action. Following the work of T. R. Young and Garth Massey, she demonstrates the effects of a dramaturgical society on rituals. The structure of everyday life in a dramaturgical society is manipulated by elites who control symbols and images of the self and community that are incorporated into ritual events and products. Deegan examines two major categories of American ritual life: *participatory rituals* and *media-created rituals* that I employ here (see discussions of concepts in chapter 1).

As there are definite rules to follow and "scripts" for every aspect of the Miss America program (in the roles of contestant, volunteer, administrator, journalist, or even as an observer), this theoretical perspective is a concise framework in which to examine the Miss America "mystique." The program's rituals can be loosely scripted and frequently performed—which is characteristic of both the local pageant scene (there are thousands of local pageants all over the country throughout the year) and of participatory rituals in general. Or, they can be tightly scripted, carefully produced, and performed by special actors witnessed by others. For example, the global telecast of the Miss America Pageant each September, a media-constructed ritual, has rehearsals and professional performances. The sharp precision with which the Miss America Pageant program exemplifies both categories solidifies its status as an American ritual drama—regardless of its various self-declared purposes such as educational advancement and personal growth.

THE MISS AMERICA PAGEANT AS A PARTICIPATORY RITUAL

Each characteristic element of a participatory ritual is an integral part of the Miss America Pageant. Face-to-face participatory interaction is present in all aspects of preparation for competition and in the actual phases of the competition itself. Contestants, volunteers, and administrators all interact with one another at meetings, rehearsals, and public appearances as the pageant comes together. During the actual categories of competition, contestants interact with volunteers, administrators, and each other backstage (literally and dramaturgically) and sometimes on-stage. But the contestants' most significant, face-to-face interactions at this point are with the panel of strangers who select the winner.

Contestants, volunteers, and administrators are constantly situated socially in a matrix of roles, social statuses, and culture; none of which is flexible or negotiable. Any rumblings of behavior exhibited by any of the above-mentioned players that would be construed as improper by the public could potentially create havoc—jeopardizing the program's reputation and quite possibly its financial sponsorship—without which there is no program. This is where the "rules for ritual action" first come into play.

From the local to the national level, the Miss America Pageant is organized by a set of rules for ritual action from start to finish. Regardless of whether you attend a local, state, or even the national Miss America finals in Atlantic City, what you see and the order in which you see it is precisely the same. The contestants *always* have their interviews with the judges prior to finals night.

When the pageant starts, the first field of competition is physical fitness in a swimsuit, followed by talent, and concluding with on-stage personality in evening wear (a floor-length gown is no longer a requirement for competition—even at the national level). For any pageant whose number of contestants require that the competition be split into preliminary nights followed by a final competition night—"finals night" begins by announcing the top ten semifinalists (nine, if there are fewer than 20 contestants, total). Those contestants who are chosen as semifinalists will have the scores from their preliminary swimsuit, talent, and on-stage personality in evening-wear competitions thrown out: The interview scores are the only numbers that carry over to finals night. The semifinalists then compcte in all three of the earlier phases of competition again, and the judges score them individually (not comparatively) with a whole number from 1 (as the lowest) to 10 (as the highest). The auditors then tally the scores, tossing out the high and the low score, as in Olympic Games. Emcees will announce any special category award winners such as the overall talent winner or the overall interview winner, and the names of the runners-up. The new "Miss Whatever" will be crowned—quite possibly to a tremendously cheesy and borderline-nauseating song—and if there's a runway, she will walk it. And with that, the "Miss Whatever Pageant" for that particular year concludes. This is *the way it is* all across America.

But contestants are not the only ones who execute rituals. For instance, it is both interesting and amusing to observe and compare seasoned pageant *audiences* with those less familiar with the nuances and subtleties of the pageant world. In Atlantic City, the Convention Hall audience of the national pageant knows that it is always proper and respectful to stand for the reigning Miss America whenever she is first introduced during a program: It is as automatic to them as it is for most Americans to salute the flag. Likewise, the majority of audience members at any of the 50 state pageants know to stand for their reigning "Miss State" when she is first introduced, as well. At local pageants, especially if each pageant has not been around long enough to become a community institution, audience members often look around in temporary bewilderment when scattered people (usually pageant volunteers and administrators) stand up for the local reigning "Miss Whatever." More amusing still, these audience members frequently are even *more* bewildered when they realize for whom everyone *is* standing, usually expecting that the ovation must be for the mayor or some other community dignitary.

THE MISS AMERICA PAGEANT AS A MEDIA-CONSTRUCTED RITUAL

On 11 September 1954 the Miss America Pageant was broadcast nationally—live on television—for the first time. This simple act did more than broaden the pageant's immediate audience: It effectively assured the program's eternal and complete dependence on corporate sponsorship for funding. An estimated 27 million viewers in approximately 8,714,000 homes watched for the first time as Miss America 1955, Lee Ann Meriwether, announced (Riverol 1992, 55). Having gained an impressive 39-percent share of the home audience (DeFord 1971, 193), from that date until the present, the Miss America Pageant has been constructed and often influenced by professionals in the mass-media industry.

Two recent events illustrate this control. In the early 1990s, the time limit for the talent competition for each contestant was cut from 2:50 to 2:30 minutes because the producers of the telecast thought it would keep the pageant within its allotted timeframe and assist in "moving the show along." This was a source of great angst to many contestants, because the talent competition is the most heavily weighed category in the judging process (40 percent) and because thousands of women all across the nation had already invested in tape recordings of music for their talent presentations timed to 2:50 minutes. Many of these timed routines could not be edited to the new time limit.

Still another media decision was to stop announcing, during the national telecast, the eight contestants who are nonfinalist talent winners. So far, none of the pageant's non-media organizers has carried enough weight to sway either of these decisions, although many people—including me—disagree with these decisions and feel that they detract from our program.

The Miss America telecast's ratings are the lifeline that connects the pageant and its sponsors. These ratings have a higher priority than the pageant establishment's desire to preserve the integrity of its program. Debra Deitering, both an advertising and marketing professional and a former Miss Iowa, states that

ten years of experience and hindsight have enlightened me to the special intro-duction Miss America gave me to big-time business, image, politics and corporate hidden agendas. I'd intuitively known and felt things going on around me, but lacked the experience and wisdom to put the pieces together. When I encountered these elements again in the business world, I began to understand my Miss America experience with greater clarity. (personal communication with author)

The national pageant is presented as a participatory ritual to a live audience in Convention Hall in Atlantic City and as a media-constructed ritual to an international television audience. NBC personnel and na-tional administrators spend months to ensure that neither audience is neglected. Although the organization of the "product" and its presenta-tion varies with each type of ritual, both rituals culminate in announcing the new Miss America, who is crowned while an undeniably cheesy song is sung in her honor.

The words to this song speak eloquently to the goals and symbols asso-ciated with the pageant. One woman each year symbolizes "your ideal." When this song is sung, the "new reigning queen" walks that fabled Con-vention Hall runway, as many before her have done, and returns to the stage ready and willing to embrace a completely altered state of exis-tence for the next 365 days of her national reign. This ideal female "aris-tocracy" fulfills the fairy-tale visions of European stories that are still being told to little girls in a nation that was founded in opposition to such undemocratic structures.

THE MISS AMERICA PAGEANT PROGRAM AS AN INSTITUTIONAL STRUCTURE IN AMERICAN SOCIETY

Deegan's *American Ritual Dramas* illustrates how most modern ritu-als are intertwined with bureaucracies, family "fun," and loyalty to the government (Deegan 1989a, 10). The Miss America Pageant Program is an examplar of these processes. For example, when contestants are asked why they participate in the program, their answers vary: Some need the scholarship money; some want the opportunity to finely hone and perfect their performing talent; and some are influenced by family members or friends. But a great many contestants say they compete sim-ply because "it's fun." This seemingly simple and honest response assumes deeper meaning when one considers the answer from a theoretical standpoint.

In *American Ritual Dramas*, the term "fun" refers specifically to an American experience that emerges from particular American rituals. Because of the structured nature of "good times" in America, many enjoyable experiences are generated in contexts of discrimination and technological control.

Fun may help the individual feel at home with a select group of others: family, friends, sorority sisters, the in-group or the team. But the wider community—those different from the self and the self's emotionally attached others—is not incorporated. (Deegan 1989a, 26)

It is not unusual for pageant participants to get caught up in the "flow" of the entire pageant process: They lose contact with ordinary reality, they experience heightened sensory appreciation, and they lose touch with the ordinary passage of time and space (see Czikzentmihalyi 1975). During the flow, a person is taken out of her "natural attitude" and experiences another reality—an "extraordinary reality" (Deegan 1989a, 26). Flow may help individuals create beautiful worlds of fantasy, equality, and communal meaning. Thriving examples of flow in the Miss America Pageant system are

1. the celebrity status of the contestants, especially for the winners who are crowned at the local, state or national level;
2. the changed, everyday reality of the titleholders when they focus on fulfilling their obligations as "Miss Whatever" and polish their competitive abilities for the next level of competition;
3. the identity-enhancing titles such as "Miss Whatever Contestant," "Miss Whatever," "Executive Director," "President," and "Hostess"; and
4. membership in what is loosely referred to as "the Miss America Family," and being entitled to the benefits of prestige and fellowship this offers.

In the scope of the Miss America spectrum, the instances when everyday reality retreats and flow prevails are virtually endless.

Although some people consider certain aspects of the whole process silly, which is not altogether unjustified, is there anything inherently wrong with any of these enjoyable experiences? For many contestants, the program delivers a number of the rewards it claims to offer: scholarship money, personal development, confidence, and self-actualization. The relationships that the Miss America program participants form with one another in all their various roles are valuable beyond price for many people. But flow is also the key component to a darker aspect of the Pageant world, one that is tremendously difficult to address and eliminate.

The flow phenomenon that lures and holds the various contestants, directors, volunteers, coaches, and other individuals immersed in the pageant system may also attract them to the potentially damaging purpose of meeting a desperate need for something tangible and measurable to define themselves and their worth. These volatile emotional dynamics, thrown into the ritual mix at virtually all levels and in all aspects of participation, can inflict significant harm on those who feel a lowered sense of self-perception and personal value.

Such people include the contestants for whom Pageant participation defines their lives instead of enhancing them—for example, the "pageant mothers" whose blind ambition for their daughters to win does not mask the fact that they want the title for themselves as much as for their daughters (maybe more). Or, the directors, coaches, and trainers whose commitment to having "this year's winner" outweighs their commitment to their titleholder's opinions, interests, personal goals, and sometimes even their physical and mental well-being. Thus, contestants can experience undue pressure to meet unrealistic weight/physical criteria and experience excessive overtraining. In short, contestants can be programmed to be walking, talking Miss America machines to fit a narrowly defined ideal.

Perhaps one of the most visible examples of flawed fun can be seen at the Southern States Ball. This is an elaborate, invitation-only affair hosted annually in Atlantic City on the Friday evening preceding Saturday's final night of national competition. At the Southern States Ball, the Miss America elite gather in an environment of enviable grace and elegance, to be greeted by men in Confederate uniform and serenaded by renditions of "Dixie" (Deitering 1994, 23). Yes—this function really does exist, and there are those for whom being granted the right to attend really is a treasured experience. This "liminal" event, however is not contemporary; it emerges from a defeated social and state structure that intended to preserve slavery and the ideals of a whites-only society.

REFLECTIONS ON MY PAGEANT PARTICIPATION RITUALS

My own experiences of being a contestant were codified by frames (Goffman 1974) that exhibited "anti-structure" (Deegan 1989a, 14). The rituals surrounding the state competitions function like a "total institution" (Goffman 1961) where "power in total institutions is organized bureaucratically, spatially, temporally and hierarchically to control every aspect of self-definition and daily rituals" (Deegan 1989a, 17). Recalling the environment in which I was completely immersed as a contestant throughout the second week of June during 1990, 1991, and 1992 (the years I participated in the Miss America Pageant at the state level in Nebraska), I recognize—with the sudden and instant clarity of recognition—the parallels between that environment and other "total institutions" described by Goffman; that is, asylums, prisons, and military boot camps. These other institutions, it is important to note, are not considered "fun," and participation is often involuntary.

On Sunday afternoon of pageant week, all incoming Miss Nebraska contestants report at a specified time to the high school auditorium in North Platte, Nebraska.[2] At this time, all contestants take part in the sign-in ceremony that marks the official beginning of pageant week. Prior to this event, all contestants are informed that members of the media and various local dignitaries will attend the sign-in ceremony. Each contestant is asked to present herself to show that she *knew* they would be there—looking and behaving as the general public expects a Miss Nebraska contestant to look and behave.

The concept behind this directive is theoretically defined as "institutional reflexivity," a social pattern or convention that confirms gender stereotypes and the prevailing arrangement between the sexes (Goffman 1974). The Miss America Pageant as an American ritual is, by virtue of its roles and rules, an exemplar of this concept. "The gender-specific clothing in the Miss America Pageant, particularly bathing suits, high heels and evening gowns are specific to the pageant, but serve to reinforce stereotypic, socially constructed gender ideals" (Deegan 1989a, 22). While the Miss Nebraska Pageant administrators never explicitly stated that the contestants should "arrive looking like Miss America," this is definitely the meaning that the majority of the pageant participants presume.

Following the afternoon's ritual sign-in activities, each contestant must read, sign, and have notarized their official state contestant contract (in which she swears, among other things, that she is a female and has *always been* a female) to secure her competitive eligibility. The contestant then follows her host-parents to their home.

The "childlike" contestant drives to the host-parents' home in her car, where she parks it until the following Sunday, after she concludes all phases of the state pageant. Contestants must not drive anywhere during pageant week for any reason. In fact, they are actually supposed to give their car keys to their host-parents to hold until pageant week is officially over. (Though, in the three years that I competed, I stayed with two different host-families, and neither of them ever made an issue of this—quite possibly because I was 23, 24, and 25 years old when I competed at the state level.)

Contestants are not to leave the homes of their host-families without a parent member of the host-family present. Host families provide transportation to rehearsals at the high school each morning and to all evening commitments and competitions. Each contestant's assigned hostess is then responsible for bringing the contestant home from these events. During rehearsals or functions, contestants are to go nowhere—including the BATHROOM—without being escorted by their hostess. Only when pageant week is over, and a new Miss Nebraska has been named can the rest of the contestants reclaim their normal lives. As for the new Miss Nebraska, winning the title extends her weeklong lease to a year, and life as she once knew it will never be the same again.

The personal and structural intricacies inherent in the Miss America Pageant involve and affect behind-the-scenes participants as well as contestants: directors, administrators, volunteers, parents, siblings, and friends. Nearly anyone with whom pageant participants have any contact or connection have the potential to be "swept in" to ritual process.

Deegan's analysis of *Star Trek* as a media-constructed ritual turned participatory ritual discusses a similar process that occurs when some fans at conventions dress and speak like their favorite fantasy figures and re-create various storylines of their choice (Deegan 1989a, 155). Many Miss Wanna-Be's permeate the Miss America Pageant as well. All too frequently, behind a sleekly groomed, highly competitive pageant contestant is a mother, director, friend, sibling, or other such person living vicariously through the contestant's trials and triumphs on the pageant stage. Most tragic of all are the contestants, reinforced with zealous support and encouragement, who *do not like* the pageant. The reluctant contestant participates because a significant other pressures her to enter.

THE MISS AMERICA PAGEANT PROGRAM'S POTENTIAL FUTURE INFLUENCE ON AMERICAN SOCIAL CULTURE

Although the Miss America Pageant defines itself as an advocate for women's empowerment—and has publically made significant strides to tailor itself to that ideal throughout its history—will this uniquely American ritual ever be a truly liberating experience for women? This may well depend on how broadly any person pondering the issue is willing to define "liberating."

Sexism and classism are two major hallmarks of a capitalist society and an integral part of the Miss America program. Sexism will most likely always remain on some level. Although the majority of the 1995 viewing audience who called to vote on whether to retain or eliminate the swimsuit competition opted in favor of retaining it, I predict that it will ultimately prove to be more trouble than it's worth. What I do not see happening is the pageant becoming a coed event, another change some have suggested. I believe that in the eyes of the participants—as well as its sponsors, and the nation at large—it will always be the "*Miss* America program." It is a female ideal of beauty and self presentation.

Classism, too, will always be a predominant part of the equation: The priorities of corporate sponsors combined with their emphasis on television ratings will always prevail over the voices of pageant participants—the volunteers or administrators of the program. The Miss America Pageant will never be free of its dependency on commercial sponsorship: It needs the sponsorship that only Chevrolet, Fruit of the Loom, and other big business, international conglomerates can provide to keep the "Miss America Machine" going. And *any* titleholder in the program is an official representative of these corporate entities. She is not only expected to, but also legally contracted and obligated to, uphold the social standards of her local, state, and national program sponsors. While the pageant's official bylaws do not forbid contestants to have purple-dyed hair or pierced noses, those who are serious about succeeding in the program are well aware of the standards they must display if they want to wear the winning crown (Deitering 1994, 21).

CONCLUSION

While I understand and appreciate the various and diverse views of the program advanced by advocates and opponents, I am confident that there will always be a Miss America Scholarship Pageant Program, and there will always be room for further improvement of this American ritual drama.

NOTES

1. The people involved in the production of the Miss America contests refer to themselves as part of the "Miss America Scholarship Pageant Program." In everyday life this is often shortened to the "Miss America Pageant" when referring to the actual final program (partially televised) with contestants from each state, and to the contests similar to it on a local level. The "Miss America Pageant Program" refers here to the advisers, judges, "alumni" of pageants, host families, paid staff, and volunteer fundraisers who do not participate as contestants in the pageants now but do participate in a wide range of activities surrounding the pageants.

2. North Platte holds Nebraska's state Miss America Scholarship Pageant Program franchise. The Miss Nebraska Scholarship Pageant has been held in North Platte since 1986 and will continue to be held there unless the national board has what they deem to believe "just cause" to move the franchise to another Nebraska community, or North Platte informs the national board that they would like to relinquish it.

IV

American Rituals and Globalization

6

The Americanization of Ritual Culture: The "Core Codes" in American Culture and the Seductive Character of American "Fun"

Mary Jo Deegan

The international hegemony of American popular culture became firmly established early in the twentieth century. For example, in 1930, Jane Addams, the American sociologist who headed the social settlement Hull-House in Chicago and who won the Nobel Peace Prize in 1931 (Deegan 1988a), recalled being introduced to a man in Tokyo. The man did not know about her decades of work for peace, but he did recognize Chicago from its image in American movies: "Chicago," he said, "oh yes; that is where they pursue the thief over the tops of roofs" (Addams 1930b, 819).

Forty years later, in 1972, I had a similar experience. I was then a doctoral student at the University of Chicago, vacationing in Germany. On several occasions when I was introduced in Germany, men pointed their fingers as if holding up imaginary pistols and said, knowingly, "Chicago, bang! bang!" The widespread export of and the joking familiarity with the Chicago gangster image[1] around the world is, of course, but one of myriad examples of the international Americanization of culture during the twentieth century.[2]

I begin this chapter, however, by noting that the long-established pattern of American cultural influence is changing in several nontrivial ways. First, the modern cultural scene is witness to many new forms of media, including cassette tapes and dual tape-deck boom boxes, VCRs, music videos, compact discs, Fax machines, multimedia home computers, the Internet, and cable and satellite television channels. Together they accelerate the mass global distribution of cultural goods (see chapters 2 and 3 for further discussions of these media changes). One result is the rapid, international proliferation of new music and dance styles. (In fact, the analysis of "the Americanization of culture" must also take into account the simultaneous influence of other national cultures, especially Latinization and Africanization, on American popular music.)

Second, the U.S.A. is now only one capitalist nation in competition with others, instead of being the dominant one. American capital no longer controls significant sectors of the ostensibly American mass-media industry. Third, many nations are producing and promoting their own forms of mass media, thereby contributing to international culture and creating new markets. Fourth, "hyper-modern" (Giddens 1990) societies are generating cultural artifacts that are increasingly divorced from traditional worldviews. In sum, the technological, economic, international, and social contexts that comprise "the Americanization of culture" are significantly altered from what they were only two decades ago when friendly Germans greeted me with stereotypical references to Chicago gangsterism.

The American culture industry is, however, responding to these changed circumstances. Specifically, the U.S.A. creates images, symbols, and experiences that are (I believe, perniciously) adapted to the worldwide alienation, repression, and oppression generated by hyper-modern situations. Recent American exports continue the global diffusion of distorting cultural imagery that Jane Addams noted in 1930, but that process has been transformed by today's economic realities.

American culture is marketed on a capitalist basis, as in the past, but Americans are losing control of the global market, both as consumers and producers. In response to this transformed market, the cultural products of the American mass media now combine patterns of structural inequality with unauthentic experiences to generate what I call "fun" (Deegan 1989a). The marketing of fun is big business, and the American mass-media industry is particularly well positioned for its exploitation. But there is more at stake here than profits and the hegemonic export of cultural imagery. The juxtaposition and packaging of everyday inequality with entertainment creates a powerful allegiance to complex forms of hyper-modern social control to which I take critical exception.

In the balance of this chapter, I first outline a theory of contemporary American fun that I call "the Americanization of ritual culture." It is my view that cultural analysis must proceed theoretically as well as empirically (many postmodern theorists appear to be independent of empirical reality—an approach antithetical to that adopted here). I then present American and European examples of the merchandising of fun in the Disney amusement package. Finally, I return briefly to my discussion above, underscoring the deep changes in the economic structure of the

American mass media. I conclude with my assessment of the potential for an international and more liberating world culture as an alternative to the incorporation and spread of structural inequalities presently championed by the global marketing of fun.

THE "CORE CODES" IN AMERICAN CULTURE AND THE SEDUCTIVE CHARACTER OF AMERICAN FUN

Hyper-modern life in the U.S.A. is driven by "core codes" that structure a wide range of cultural patterns, from fleeting, face-to-face interactions to enduring, large-scale social institutions (chapter 1). These codes give recognizable contours to hyper-modern American cultural rituals, especially the combination of participatory and media-constructed rituals. Two such combinations, Disneyland Paris (DLP) and McDonald's, are discussed here. American rituals of both types are intended to be part of leisure life, and, therefore, they are seen as less serious than work. They generate a typical experience called "fun." The seductive character of fun emerges from its predictable capacity to generate short-lived, incomplete escapes from mundane routine. In the process, fun simultaneously strengthens and reproduces the core oppressions and repressions of everyday life.

The new Americanization of culture is accelerated everywhere when fun-generating ritual culture from the U.S.A. is marketed globally. At stake here is not the simple merchandizing of fun, but the simultaneous mass export of the core codes that make fun ever more attractive. Remember, to "have fun" American-style is concurrently to acknowledge the everyday validity of the core codes that give fun its experiential meaning. Under the guise of good-natured fun and harmless "good times," the marketing of American ritual culture such as DLP and McDonald's covertly reinforces the predatory American core codes that make fun seductive to consumers and profitable to investors.

DISNEYLAND PARIS IS NOT ENJOYABLE BUT IT SURE IS FUN

DLP generated considerable public debate in France when it opened ("Farmers Protest at Euro Disneyland" 1992). This controversy emerged in part because DLP differs from prior forms of the Americanization of culture that have been incorporated into the European experience. The history of the Americanization of culture in Europe primarily involved media-constructed rituals. DLP, however, combines the powerful mass media of Disney films, videos, cassettes, books, and toys with the participatory ritual experienced by Americans in similar Disney-defined theme parks in the U.S.A. The mass marketing of Disney products is so widespread that many rest stops along turnpikes in Germany, Austria, and Hungary carry such products for sale.

The Disney experience is rooted in hyper-modern ritual and specifically responds to the alienation rampant in American life. This results in huge profits. The Disney enterprise maintains capitalist control over rituals that are not playful for children nor for parents.

The Project on Disney (1995) documented the wide range of problems facing life "inside the [Mickey] mouse." Alienated, underpaid workers who cannot unionize characterize the backstage of employment as "working at the rat" (pp. 110–62), and hiding deep social problems at the parks—such as rapes, kidnappings, and muggings—requires a massive backstage management (pp. 52–53). Even normal problems such as serious illness and death are erased from everyday life at the capitalist, bureaucratic "Magic" place.

One participant in this Project on Disney, Susan Willis, noted many examples of core codes. She wrote: "Organizing a family vacation to Disney World demands managerial and economic decision-making skills equal to those required by big business" (Willis 1995, 34–35). People trade "time for money" and, she reflects, "actually, it's hard to imagine a spontaneous vacation anywhere" (p. 36). In this setting, "shopping is a ride not unlike the other amusements" (p. 40), and participation feels like being in a large video game (p. 37, see chapter 3 here).

An article in the *Chicago Tribune* by Eileen Ogintz (1992) also illustrates the problematic nature of the Disney ritual. Ogintz is a mother who traveled with her husband and three children to Disney World in Florida. She discusses the American Disney experience in terms of tips she learned for surviving the episode. Her first tip is that the ordeal is not relaxing; her second tip is that it is expensive—costing more than (U.S.) $400 for four-day passes for a family of four in 1992. Ogintz (1992, 8) literally calls the trip fun and writes: "Keep reminding yourself that you're there to enjoy. That's what I kept reminding my husband as we waited in line for 30 minutes to ride a three-minute attraction, stood watching a parade in the rain and shelled out money for everything." Meals, lodging, and souvenirs are additional. Ogintz notes that it costs (U.S.) $120 for a meal and tickets to the Hoop-De-Doo Theater, and (U.S.) $34 for a bland breakfast Ogintz served to her increasingly sullen children. Ogintz writes that she does not want to repeat the experience, but—importantly—*her children do*. Thus, she concludes with pseudo-humor, it was "worth it."

Why was such an expensive and clearly unenjoyable experience "worth it" to Ogintz and millions of other Americans, Japanese, and Europeans?[3] This is the conundrum I wish to understand and partially explain through the theory of core codes. In sum, I conclude that the "Disney experience" is characterized by class codes, bureaucratization, sexism, hyper-modern use of time, and, of course, the fun that is intrinsically alienating yet seductive. DLP is an important target for social protests and for study by scholars because it is an American vision funded by American dollars and is an imported composite of participatory and mass-media rituals (see chapter 7 here). A similar powerful American media-constructed and participatory ritual is found globally with the McDonald's franchise.

"TAKING A BREAK TODAY" WITH FAST FOODS

Other American rituals are also international while they remain substantially in American control. For example, the fast food industry and the subsequent "McDonaldization" of food is transforming eating habits, diet, and social interactions throughout the world. The fast food ritual, characterized by assembly-line work methods in an industry that sells friendliness in service delivered by a low-paid, unorganized work force and food that is often fried and high in fat content, has the potential to change numerous personal, participatory rituals such as birthdays, holidays, and family dinners, as well.

The quick adoption of McDonald's in hyper-modern, capitalist societies is easily understandable in Western European countries and the British Western allies that share many core codes with the U.S. It is surprising, however, to see the rapid growth of this industry in the former Soviet Union and in Hong Kong before it reverted to Chinese control.

McDonald's is experiencing its greatest profits in countries outside the U.S.A. By the end of 1996, the corporation projected almost two-thirds of its new outlets in foreign locations (Samuels 1996). The "McDonald's culture" is explicit and depends on a relatively low price for a product that is delivered quickly and reliably by labor that is not unionized. Franchisees, managers, and assistant managers are taught this culture in "Hamburger Universities" located in the U.S.A., Germany, the United Kingdom, and Japan. One author believes this is such a sure-fire marketing program that "if McDonald's builds its own Starship and sends it on a five-year mission: 'To seek new life and civilization,'" it would be able "to boldly go where no hamburger has gone before'" (J. Wayne cited in Salva-Ramirez 1995, 19).[4]

The prepackaged fast food experience is part of a process that is no longer American *per se*; it flourishes in market-driven economies uncontrolled by any one government or culture. It is hyper-modern life at its most frightening peak. Such "pure" American products and commodities are, however, rare in contemporary society—our next topic of discussion.

THE CHANGING MYTH OF THE AMERICANIZATION
OF CULTURE

Most blockbuster American films—with big stars, multimillion-dollar funding, and huge box office receipts—are no longer simply American media-constructed rituals. They emerge from an international marketplace; celebrity roster; and combination of writers, directors, and producers. They are intentionally (Schutz 1967, 1971) made for a global market. They appear to be American, but this is often a dramaturgical presentation (Goffman 1959) of an American ritual. In other words, these new films present the front but not the substance of an American ritual. The financiers, directors, writers, and actors, for example, are not necessarily Americans, but they are able to create a cultural product that appears to be American.

Even indigenous American rituals, like rap music, are rapidly transformed by their appearance on an international stage. Thus, many music industries in different countries have transformed rap music into their own musical style and presentation. American rap, for example, is often an African-American music that explores the black experience of poverty, alienation, violence, and racism. I saw Italian "rappers" on television in 1991, however, who wore a type of cheerleader's outfit, had a "cheery and upbeat" style of self-presentation, and were on mainstream television. What kind of transformations occurred with such a different context? It is hard to enumerate the multiplicity of differences between African-American rap and this form of Italian rap.

In addition, the French now suffer from the successful structure of the American package of creating films. In 1983, the French Minister of Culture, Jack Lang, instituted a series of social changes to fight the overwhelming power of the American cinema in France. Lang fostered establishment of two production units, now called Ciby 2000 and Studio Canal-Plus. These businesses, controlled and funded by the French, are now so successful, however, that independent filmmakers and directors in France fear their indigenous powers in the cinematic industry (Chutrow 1992).

Finally, in an increasingly nontraditional world, rituals have no fixed ownership or control by everyday people. These rapidly transformed products are in many ways culturally anonymous. Any hyper-modern or modernizing society can use them, change them, or discard them with relative ease. We see this flexibility in a craze in Japan over the television series *Twin Peaks*. I briefly summarize this phenomenon.

Twin Peaks as an Example of the Adaptability of American Rituals

Twin Peaks was an American television series with a complicated, mystical plot, and unusual (for American TV) characters. David Lynch, the producer, director, and sometimes author of the series, presented his view of small-town life in America as secretive, sexually degenerate, violent, and bizarre beneath an appearance of natural beauty, serenity, and friendliness. One frequent image in the series was the cyanotic, murdered, plastic-wrapped corpse of a young woman, Laura Palmer. The series' thematic question was "Who Killed Laura Palmer?"

This view of American life was wildly popular for a short time in 1991, but audience support continued to dwindle after the first season. It was a fad that did not last and even became boring to many Americans.[5] This American rejection, however, did not occur in Japan.

The cancelled television series was made into a movie, funded by France's Ciby 2000 (Chutrow 1992). The film was first released in Japan in mid-May 1992, and sold strongly there. Its success emerged from the highly successful marketing of the television series on pay television in Japan. By 1992 the entire series had aired six times in Japan, and there was a 26-hour marathon that showed all episodes uninterrupted. Videotapes of the series sold for £440 apiece, and 15,000 copies were bought. People waited in long lines to rent the series. Buying and eating favorite foods used on the show, taking expensive trips to the U.S.A., joining fan clubs for the series' actors, and buying and making macabre photographs of young Japanese women wrapped in plastic and posing in coffins were further signs of the *Twin Peaks* mania (Pollack 1992).

This Japanese phenomenon is particularly hard to explain because, according to leading Japanese film critic Makoto Takimoto: "I don't think, generally speaking, that David Lynch's view of the world fits into Japanese feeling." Makoto does not understand how this situation emerged. I, however, offer this explanation: the seductiveness of fun. Japan is a society that retains a mixture of traditional and hyper-modern ways. Hyper-modern patterns are dramatically changing traditional Japanese mores, nonetheless. American mass-media rituals and fast foods are providing models of behavior that are simultaneously attractive to and destructive of Japanese society. Such massive uprooting of social values will continue throughout our increasingly global society. These changes, however, could be liberating instead of destructive. It is the potential for a new, liberating ritual world that I discuss next.

LIBERATING RITUALS AND THE WEAVING OF A NEW, GLOBAL RITUAL TAPESTRY

The proliferation of new forms of mass media, funding, travel, and cultural visions need not remain tied to structural inequality and the experiences they generate. Playfulness abandons the repressions and oppressions of the American core codes. We can learn to play with new possibilities and visions on a global scale. The new world and consciousness is international (Deegan 1992b). I see this new vision with the emerging potential of the European Community, the dismantling of the Eastern bloc and the former Soviet Union, and even, to a degree, the global blockbuster phenomenon. Satellite radio and television as well as computers are also exciting new tools.

What is needed to foster this world community are structural patterns that control and limit the destructive core codes embedded in American rituals and fun. These would include generating social rules eliminating, or at least ameliorating, the repressive and oppressive effects of core codes. These rules would respond to differences and be emancipatory in intent and practice.

Emancipatory rituals generate community bonds, shared experiences that reveal our shared lives. Emancipatory rituals play with everyday structures. They allow us

to laugh at ourselves, disregard our divisions, and enact topsy-turvy rules. . . . Ideas controlled by the people and enriched by their creative energy and technological skills can yield new forms of celebration that learn from the past, build a meaningful present, and generate anticipation of a joyful future. (Deegan 1989a, 161)

This new world requires hope and leadership, resistance and creativity, scholarship and action. It is clear that, collectively, we can create alternative futures and optional cultures (Giddens 1987). A portion of this possibility is revealed in my work here: a collective voice for the possibility of a world we neither knew in the past nor can foresee in our immediate future.

CONCLUSION

American culture is a powerful, but flawed, force throughout the world. Its influence in the film industry has flourished for most of this century. Significant, recent changes in this process have emerged due to the many new forms of mass media, the growing worldwide capitalist market and declining financial control of the U.S.A. in the 1980s and 1990s, and the increasing power of nations everywhere to create their own contributions to mass media. Hyper-modernity has generated cultural artifacts that are increasingly divorced from a traditional worldview; but conscious, democratic decisions concerning community rituals are both possible and desirable.

Recent cultural commodities and experiences exported from the U.S.A.; or ostensibly from the U.S.A.; have led to considerable debate, consternation, and profits. I argue here that American rituals incorporate oppressive and repressive core codes amid problematically enjoyable experiences called fun. The power of combining structural discrimination and fun in these situations must be increasingly under-stood and resisted, both within the U.S.A. and elsewhere. By contrast, emancipatory rituals that embrace an international horizon are within the reach of all democratic communities.

NOTES

1. The equally serious proliferation of violent crimes in other cities, for example: Detroit, New York, and Washington, D.C., have done little to displace the enduring media image of Chicago as the crime capital of the U.S.A. Of course, Miami and Los Angeles have images of being "crime capitals," but this image is often gritty and controlled by heinous drug lords who are not admired as American gangsters. Washington, D.C., is often depicted as the home of big crooks in the government, but this, too, is not the gangster image.

2. Michael R. Hill and I were struck, for example, to note (during our 1980 visit) the numerous instances of American cultural influence in Cuba despite the general anti-American stance of the Cuban government (Deegan 1981; Hill 1981, 1983).

3. See Borcover (1992) for a discussion of European workers' quick adaptation to DLP's employment expectations and conditions, including dress codes and corporate behavioral norms.

4. This quotation is obviously a play on words of the *Star Trek* formula, a good example of an Amercan ritual echo (Deegan 1989a).

5. *TV Guide*, a popular weekly magazine, selected a panel to make a list of the "100 Greatest Episodes of All Time" (1997). Those experts selected one episode of *Twin Peaks* out of tens of thousands of competitors to rank as the 25th best episode. This winner was the opening hour of the series. This suggests that the series may become a cult classic despite its general rejection by American audiences.

7

American Ritual Drama in Action: The Disney Theme Park

Yochanan Altman

The opportunity accorded to us with the opening of the Disney theme park in Paris in April 1992,[1] currently known as Disneyland Paris (DLP),[2] to examine the workings of an American icon outside its natural habitat has been too great a temptation to resist. Perhaps this has been more fascinating since its first three years of operation resulted in unprecedented losses—against expectations and contrary to earlier results in the three other theme parks in Anaheim, California; Orlando, Florida; and Tokyo, Japan. We discuss these issues, and its particularly cold reception in France, elsewhere (Altman 1995; Altman and Jones, 1992, 1993). Here, we are concerned with Deegan's (1989a) theory of American core codes and their expressions in everyday life events. We wish to highlight some features of the Disney experience, because we believe, like the French philosopher Jean Baudrillard (1988, 28), "that the whole of the Western world is hypostatised in America, the whole of America in California, and California in Disneyland. . . . [T]his is the microcosm of the West."

We use as our main observation post the theme park in Paris, but we have followed closely the other theme parks, either personally and/or through our associates and students, and what we say is applicable to any of the four theme parks. Not only do they resemble each other remarkably (Altman 1995), but all their designs, principles of operation, services, and products are one and the same.

DISNEYLAND PARIS (DLP)

DLP is the largest theme park and recreation complex in Europe, encompassing some 600 hectares (1,482 acres) of amusement attractions and 5,200 hotel rooms in Marne-Vallée on the outskirts of Paris. Modeled on the first Disney theme park in California, it is the latest addition to the theme park division of the Disney empire and its second foreign venture after Tokyo Disneyland. More than 10,000 people on average operate it (there are seasonal variations), of which 9,000 are permanent staff (Besson 1996). The overall direct capital investment by the end of 1994 was in the region of 27.7 billion francs, including local and national government investment in infrastructure ("Disneyland Paris" 1995). From its opening in April 1992 to September 1996, the park was visited by some 36 million visitors (Johnston 1996).

THE DISNEY EXPERIENCE

The Disney formula for a "quality guest experience" is defined through official language employed in advertising, staff manuals, and brochures in a language known as Disney-speak.[3] The phrase, in Disney-speak, translates into a "good value for the money." The training manual for new recruits expresses this same ideology as follows:

safety + courtesy + efficiency + show = happiness.

The secret of this succinct recipe lies in the interdependency of its elements. Take one away and the "magic experience" (Disney-speak) tumbles.

There is another part of the formula that is equally explicit. For "guest" read "guests" and more precisely read "family." The Disney theme park is designed for family entertainment. The interdependency, therefore, further extends to the target population. The children are the "pulling" force because the theme parks are often depicted as a "children's paradise." The adults, however, are the ones who pay; therefore, they too are involved.

Children are also critical elements because in advanced industrial societies only children are permitted to indulge in unrestrained, spontaneous outbursts of excitement. Adults are socialized into emotional restraint that extends into their leisure activities (Elias and Dunning 1986). To create a "party hat" atmosphere, with visitors sporting their newly acquired Mickey Mouse ears or cowboy hats, the children's presence is crucial, as they need to set the tone and provide the legitimacy for excitement.

Adults, in addition to their role as paymasters, assume the heavy burden of facilitating the "make believe" work. A smiling and happy adult makes it easier for other adults to join in the fairy-tale fantasy. Conversely, a nonsmiling adult with a somber face spells disaster. This explains why the key characteristic emphasized in recruitment is "to know how to work with a smile,"[4] and why smiling is elevated to a philosophy of work and life: "The Disney smile is not a rictus. It's just a sign of natural courtesy, a sign of knowing that you're part of a winning team, doing the best for your guests, sharing the same goals, speaking the same language" (*Disney University*, 4). Practice in the friendly smile is the first training that employees receive, and before entering the public area behind the "back stage" (Disney-speak), a note reminds the workers: "Do you know where your smile is?"[5]

In other words, the "passport" (Disney-speak for entrance ticket) to "happiness" hinges on a rather tight formula. It is tight, first, because of the interdependence of its constituent parts; and, second, because the values they transmit are a culturally constructed ritual drama (also discussed below). Tightness is, of course, the hallmark of the Disney business empire: the way the selling of its films reinforces the selling of Disney copyrighted merchandise and both form the contents of its theme parks, which in turn support the popularity of their films and associated merchandise (Grover 1991).

THE DISNEY RITUAL DRAMA

Deegan (1989a) identifies four American core codes (sex, time, class, and bureaucracy, see discussion in chapter 1). We propose that when these occur concurrently, their potency increases significantly. The genius of Walt Disney was, we believe, to design *his park* (his term) in a way that taps into these core codes by bringing them together in space and time. We propose the term "core code cluster" to refer to this amalgamation: "Core code clusters" are concrete events employing core codes in action, where all codes defined by Deegan operate concurrently, thereby reinforcing each other. As core codes are universally accepted (in a given culture) their coexistence renders the event popular and satisfying.

We focus here on the role of money to form a nucleus for a core code cluster and to show fun as a typical experience that emerges from this cluster and characterizes the Disney theme park.

MONEY

Money has emerged—for at least the past 200 years—as the key mechanism of economic life. In addition to its economic significance, money also plays a crucial social role. Indeed, one can differentiate societies on the basis of their attitude to money (Altman and Jones 1992). In the Anglo-Saxon culture, money has become the great liberator from life's constraints (Altman and Jones 1992). Spending money, therefore, is a way of manifesting this liberation.

The DLP story begins and ends with money. The greed shines through the pages of an account describing the Disney team embarking on its European venture, written by an avid sympathizer of the Walt Disney Company (Grover 1991). Maximizing potential gains, minimizing direct investment, ensuring control over copyright-merchandise franchising, and operational profits created a Disney-negotiated agreement that was a capitalist dream come true. A massive infrastructure of road and rail links, tax concessions, and land rights was underwritten by the French government, the local government, a consortium of financial institutions, and the public at large. These groups helped subsidize the profitable enterprise. Investors were invited to take part in the handout (the underwriters projected $1 billion annual profits by the mid-1990s), and the share float on the London and Paris stock exchanges was a resounding success.

Investment, enterprise, and financial risks are hallmarks of the Anglo-Saxon idea of handling money (Altman and Jones 1992; Altman and Billsberry 1994): It is a quintessential *masculine attribute* (Hofstede 1980, 1991) and thereby tied to the sex code. Making money is a fine example of *making it* in terms of success, social achievement, and personal rewards.

Money is, of course, time commodified. In America "time is money" (Deegan 1989a, 51). Indeed, beating time is the hallmark of the successful careerist—the high flyer, the fast tracker, who advances rapidly up the organizational ladder, heralding the notion that "the sky is the limit," reminiscent of another American icon—Superman (Altman 1997).[6]

Money changes hands on every corner of the park. Each ride begins and ends with its attached boutique where memorabilia, alluding to the magic moment just experienced, may be purchased. Snacks, representing most of the available food and eateries of every kind and size, sprout all over the site. Consumers are encouraged to part with their money every few yards or so, which may make the magic experience magically expensive (Ogintz 1992; Heller 1995). Indeed, the failure to allure visitors to spend more money was attributed as a main cause for the financial difficulties in the first three years of DLP's operation. In Orlando, for example, the income from the sale of food, merchandise, and hotel rooms contributes a major share to the overall profits (Fjellman 1992).

The encouragement to spend money without control alludes to a central theme of the park: its "infantilization," whereby the bureaucratic core code, with its subthemes of parent/child; control/freedom; withhold/let go; comes into operation. Infantilization is manifested throughout the theme park: in the fantasy themes (the lands), the attractions (rides), in the foods, and the merchandise. The leitmotif is universal accessibility, and therefore, a stress on the lowest-common denominator (children) is unavoidable.

INFANTILIZATION AND THE AGE CORE CODE

Although discrimination against the very young and the very old are well-known phenomenona and part of an age code (see chapter 11), adults can be treated inappropriately for their age expectations, too. When adult Disney "guests" are treated like children, their skills, choices, and intelligence are systemtically limited. To understand the infantilization of adults at DLP, it is necessary to analyze how American children are conceptualized and treated.

Of interest here is Geoffrey Gorer's (1948) portrayal of American children. This classic account reflects the prevalent conventions of white, middle America where Disney (a middle-American man himself) formulated his plans for the "Magic Kingdom." Three of Gorer's observations are of particular relevance.

First, Americans assume that "the child is born faultless, a *tabula rasa*, and any defects which subsequently develop are the fault of uncontrollable circumstances, or of the ignorance or malice of the parents who mar what [would] otherwise be a perfect, or at least perfectly adjusted, human being" (Gorer 1948, 50). The myth of childhood as the realm of the innocent and pure—merely a step away from the kingdom of fairy tales and magic—is central to the construction of Disney's theme park.

Second, there is an emphasis during early childhood on scheduled feedings and an opposition to indulged nutrition, the use of food as a reinforcer for good behavior (and food withdrawal for bad behavior), and the resultant neurotic attitude toward food satiation.[7] Practically all the food sold in the Disney theme parks is fast food (see chapter 6). Though the *fast* part of the food is important (and is discussed shortly), of interest here is the childlike quality of the foods offered. They are mostly processed and thereby easily digested; portioned for a child's grasp made with added taste enhancers (to suit a child's palate); and altogether they are rarely satisfying (thereby necessitating frequent breaks).

Third, there is an emphasis on rearing to independence, mastery of skills, and calculated risk-taking that is present from an early age.

As soon as a child has acquired sufficient physical independence to be let out of doors alone—certainly by the age of three and often earlier—it will leave its family and spend most of its time with its competitors and rivals in the immediate neighborhood . . . [the mother] should be ashamed of keeping a constant eye on the child, keeping it permanently tied to her apron strings. By so doing, she would risk committing the greatest crime which an American parent can commit: she would risk turning her child into a sissy. (Gorer 1948, 61–62)

The Disney theme park provides the decor for an illusion of independence. Some rides are designed for toddlers (age 3+), while young children can experience the thrill of driving a car on "real" roads, and teenagers are challenged to dare enter a haunted house or ride the famous Big Thunder mountain train (or the latest attraction, Space Mountain). It is a win-win game. By merely joining the ride, one is assured of completing the task successfully.

Since the theme park is based on the lowest-common denominator—a child's world—the underlying assumption has to be that adults can act like children. That is, daddy and junior can become pals for the day, and both can indulge in "Uncle Walt's" (Disney-speak) costly handouts. Infantilization is the lynch pin between a core code cluster of *money* and the creation of *fun*.

FUN AT DLP

"Fun," denoting a pleasant experience, is a key term in American everyday life (see chapter 1). "Having fun" is to leisure what "having a nice day" is to work. Significantly, the two concepts—leisure and work—are *not* opposites. The common saying of corporate America, "we work hard but we play hard," manifests this linkage.

Deegan (1989a, 26) considers fun a typical leisure experience, a by-product of hyper-modernization, which has the appearance of playfulness and "may help the individual feel at one with a select group of others; for example, family, friends, the in-group, or the team" (Deegan 1989a, 9). It is an escape from the mundane, everyday life, but it provides only a partial and limited relief (confined by time, space, and costs, among other barriers to play).

The Disney theme park is the supreme manifestation of an infantile "fun" environment. The central feature of the park is the "attractions" (rides), which may conveniently be defined here as "fun machines." A fun machine is based on providing a mostly sensual stimulation in an imaginary landscape. It is strictly commodified in time (most rides take two to three minutes), space (all are individualized),[8] and movement (one is confined to a seat and usually belted for the duration of the ride). The imagery may be rich, but it is static and strictly regulated: Everyone passes through the same routine. No variability is possible. Weber's (1958/1920) "iron cage rationality" is clearly having a field day here.

Fun "Disney style" requires being receptive to external stimuli. It is fast, it is concrete, and the point is attained in the process of "doing it." Doing more of it, presumably, is good value for money. All these behaviors are associated with masculinity (Hofstede 1980, 1991).

The emphasis on fast and concrete actions extends to other aspects of the park. The food offered is fast food, and the accent is on consuming it

quickly. Though DLP reluctantly introduced more frequently spaced restaurants and even alcohol, to placate the French and European palate,
these changes stand in opposition to the whole concept of the park. The
point in having alcohol with your meal is not the drink *per se* but the opportunity to relax. There is no idle space to be found where visitors may
relax. Space is commodified in rides, food, and merchandise. The totality
of the design allows no escape from the fantasy. To enjoy Disney, one
needs to consume in all ways. There is no relief; the background music
penetrates even the "public" toilets.

Fun means taking make-believe risks in a safe environment, thereby
playing to the angst of middle-class (notably white; see chapters 2 and 3)
America. This is manifested first and foremost in its architectural landscape. On entering the park, passing through Main Street Station, one
walks down a perfect mockup of an idealized midwestern town with a
high street from around the turn of the century: a reassuring fantasy to
an American mind.[9] "The idea of the small town has come to function in
U.S. culture as the home of nostalgia for a pre-urban America. It is the
place where harassed people in a dangerous, impersonal, and unfriendly
world can symbolically locate friendship, order, intimacy, [and] inno-
cence" (Fjellman 1992, 10).

The genius of Disney was to use this benign image, with which all
strata of society (but in particular the lower-middle classes) could identify and turn it into a "landscape of power" (Zukin 1991). Main Street
U.S.A. is the visual conduit through which visitors begin to realize the license (for which they paid) to enjoy themselves. Entry tickets are called
"passports" to sell the idea that the customer is leaving everyday life and
crossing a border into fantasy and fun.

Another major feature is "the Magic Kingdom," that is surrounded by
a ramp and dominated by three mini-diesel, fuel-burning, steam locomo-
tives from the same benign era. The train pulls open-bench carriages
named after early American cities. The rail tracks thus form a natural
fence that separates the Magic Kingdom from the outside world. This
emphasis on not allowing the outside into the park is reinforced by planning the surrounding area in such a way that does not permit the outside
scenery to be seen from inside the park—reality becomes invisible,
magical-like. The (obsessive) cleanliness of the resort, the perfect gar-
dens, the prohibition of dogs, the neatly dressed service providers, all are
designed to create "a fantasy sanctuary."[10]

Inside the sanctuary, Main Street U.S.A. leads to the central fantasy
landmark, Sleeping Beauty's Castle. This is the sex code incarnate: A
submissive, helpless female beauty is saved by the gallant, daring Prince
Charming. The tale encapsulates well the ideology of an American sex-
coded fantasy. Entry into the castle also confirms that one is at the heart
of the Magic Kingdom; having firmly left the outside, one may now pro-

ceed to the different magic lands that radiate from Sleeping Beauty's Castle,[11] mount the rides, buy souvenirs, eat snacks, see/hear/sense/touch aplenty, and have fun.

LEISURE AS CONSUMPTION

To take this deconstruction a step further, we follow Deegan's (1989a) discourse on leisure rituals, by differentiating between three levels of leisure. We call them "passive," "participatory," and "emancipatory" (for the latter term, see Deegan 1989a, 160–61) leisure rituals.[12]

Passive Leisure Rituals

This is the least-complicated (differentiated) level of leisure consumption. It denotes a simple, direct, one-to-one relationship between consumer and object. This would be the case with, for instance, movies, magazines, fashion, foods, and American classical icons such as westerns, comics, Levis, Coca-Cola, and Pepsi.

The consumer has a clear idea of what to expect based on past experience, the visibility of the product (who does not recognize a western, Levis, or Coca-Cola?), and its specificity (a movie, a pair of trousers, a refreshment). The guarantee of consistency, embedded in the product's image, adds to the simplicity and efficiency of consumption. It is a trivial event[13] in turn-of-the-century western society.

Participatory Leisure Rituals

A theme park is a more complex form of leisure consumption, not the least because it is not habitual in the way that passive consumption may be. A family trip to a Disney theme park is a planned, intentional, and infrequent occurrence.

More importantly, leisure consumption in a theme park is an *interactive* experience. It engages the customer in a hands-on experience in an essential way to make "the show work." The customer's societal assumptions and expectations meet those represented by the park's total milieu and, through that, its core codes.

Even though it promotes the notion of a family experience, the Disney theme park is evidently individually centered; and, hence, surprisingly antifamily and practically anticommunitas (see chapter 1 for a discussion of communitas). In the theme park, the main leisure interface is a person-to-object experience, mostly with a machine object or a machine-like human. Staff, of course, are not simply service providers; they are "cast members" (Disney-speak) in a grand show. Their role is specified in minutiae, particularly the Disney characters, who, like mechanical toys, may only move (but not talk) in a preprogrammed manner.

While a visit to a Disney theme park is not a daily event, *it is trivial* in that it builds on the materials of everyday life: Rides can be found in any fair, fast food on every street corner, and Disney merchandise as common as milk and bread. The Disney theme park simply provides more of the same in a condensed form for efficient consumption. It is an aggrandizement of daily life: the epitome of "have a nice day" à la Americaine (Altman and Jones 1992).

Emancipatory Leisure Rituals

As it builds on existing social structures and conventions, leisure consumption the Disney way reinforces the core codes of sex, class, bureaucracy, age, and commodified time. Since these characteristics are essentially divisive (differentiating people on the basis of gender, class, age, health, rank, and so on), the one thing the Disney experience does not do is facilitate an emancipatory experience. This experience is a more demanding form of leisure consumption because it requires a departure from the established cultural and societal norms that govern daily behavior, including consumer behavior. It stands in opposition to participatory leisure and differs from interactive consumption in that it is group-centered. Significantly, it has the potential to create play as opposed to fun (Deegan 1989a). Open to all, play is nondiscriminatory and helps break the barriers between people that are maintained by core codes. This kind of leisure has the potential to transform, and in this respect, it is emancipatory: a personalized aspect of playfulness, relaxation (as opposed to fun), and the creation of unity and reciprocity in the wider community.

Institutions of emancipatory leisure are common. The English street corner pub (particularly in its latest version, which incorporates women and children) comes readily to mind; as do its continental counterparts, for example, the south German Bierßtube, the French cafe, and the American bar (for an analysis of the meet/meat market ritual in singles bars, see Deegan 1989a). Other examples of emancipatory leisure are simple outdoor games, the French Pétanque (Boules) that can be played anywhere, major traditional calendar events such as the European Mardi Gras carnivals,[14] and religious events such as pilgrimages (see Turner and Turner 1978).

CONCLUSION

Although "the magic experience" alludes to transformation, it is *not* transformational. It cannot be for three reasons. First, the Disney theme park's design and mode of operation are a series of stimulatory interactions between a person and a machine. They may be "great fun" but they are actually stressful, emotional work. Second, because of Walt Disney's personality and the decisive impact he had on "his" park, it is highly unlikely that this obsessive-compulsive genius would have intentionally created an emancipatory event. Wallace (1985, 40) asserts that Disney "quite consciously stripped away the honky-tonk legacies of the carnival" and created a controlled, middle-class, midwestern ideal. Third, because the core code clusters are reflected in every detail of the park and milieu, they reinforce the dominant American cultural values: gender typing, time commodification, a bureaucratic-like power structure, and class differentials. Infantilization of adults exacerbates the power of this core code cluster. The "magic experience" may be an exhilarating event, but it is not an emancipatory one.

NOTES

1. DLP has been an ongoing interest of mine since its opening in April 1992. In the course of the intervening years, many people assisted me in gathering data and in generating ideas. I would like to thank, in particular, the former evening MBA students at CUBS: Thomas Yeoh, Richard Arnfield, Alex Dale, Angus Forbes, Iain Torrance, Maeve Gallagher, Kath Reddy, Douglas Lyons, John Maloney, and Pamela You; Tracy Jones from CERAM, Nice, France, who collaborated with me on two articles on the subject; Maria Morris (formerly from Sterling), and those past and present employees of DLP who helped me with invaluable insights.

2. This park was named EuroDisney (sometimes written as two words) from 1992–1994, and renamed Euro Disneyland from 1994–1995.

3. "Disney-speak" is the language taught to employees and used in internal communications within the organization. It creates a structure of thought and behavior congruent with the core codes of DLP. It is the official talk within the theme park and in formal communications (advertisements; pamphlets sold at the park, and so on).

4. The smile as a job skill was used in an advertisement in *Le Monde*, 27 April 1996, p. 82: "Even if you don't have a specialization in languages, we at Euro Disney have 1,200 different jobs to offer and the opportunities we have will be numerous for those who know how to smile in working" (author's translation).

5. This sign was shown in a British Broadcasting Company documentary, "Disney at Work," and aired on 29 April 1997.

6. Recall the moment in *Superman III* (the film sequel) when the hero stops the globe in its swivel and retrieves time so that, Orpheus-like, he can snatch his beloved Lois Lane, the ordinary American girl, from the jaws of death. The conquest of death is, of course, the ultimate conquest of time. The Superman series, like the Disney theme park, is another core code cluster of American culture.

7. Gorer employs a Freudian frame of reference. Although he does not say so, his interpretation of food-related child-rearing practices in America points to an "oral fixation" in Freudian terms. Interpreting the Disney theme park as an oral fantasy is quite possible, whereby the role of money as an oral fetish would be highlighted.

8. Even when people share a space, the experience is individualized. Thus, in the CinéMagique, a 3-D film is shown that requires the viewer to wear 3-D spectacles, thereby isolating spectators from each other. In Star Tours, though a group of some twenty people may share a "flight," the lights are off and the shared experience is therefore reduced to hearing shrieks of fright (or delight?) from others.

9. Walt Disney paid more attention to Main Street in his role as designer "supremo" than to any other feature of the park (Fjellman 1992).

10. Isn't it telling that it was a neurotic obsessive-compulsive who created the perfect "fun" concept?

11. The centrality of Sleeping Beauty's Castle in the theme park's narrative is reflected in the concentrated effort to "Frenchify" it. It is one of the few attractions formally presented in their French name: *Le Chateau de la Belle au Bois Dormant*. A long story is woven attempting to convince us that its design was influenced by a French medieval manuscript and even [surprise, surprise] the architecture of Mont-St.-Michel, a famous French landmark. The fact of the matter is that DLP's Sleeping Beauty's castle differs very little from its American equivalents.

12. Deegan (1989a, 161) defines "emancipatory rituals" as "controlled, defined, and enacted by the participants. They articulate their experience and generate the meaning of their lives in the process."

"Rituals that generate communitas must play with everyday structure." She does not focus on leisure rituals as a distinct type of ritual.

13. [I do not share this definition of these cultural objects as always trivial—ed. note.]

14. [The New Orleans Mardi Gras is patterned after the French model, but the American version is a much more capitalist enterprise. The latter event attracts hundreds of thousands of tourists who are not there to celebrate the last day before Lent but who want to "have a good time." Although the majority of tourists can enjoy this visit, the crowd can be drunk, violent, aggressive, and a dangerous experience for women. A large police presence is needed to contain this fun and protect monied consumers. Hierarchal class differences during this celebration are sharply drawn in the local community, too—ed. note.]

8

A "Christmas" Story: An Analysis of the Santa Claus Phenomenon

Sharon K. Larson

The Santa Claus phenomenon offers an engaging opportunity to examine christmas[1] in the United States as fun. In this chapter, I examine the American ritual drama of the christmas holiday season by evaluating the backstage meanings of who Santa is, where Santa lives, what Santa brings, how much Santa spends, and when Santa visits. I focus on the oppressive nature of capitalism, commodification of time, and sexism (Deegan 1989a) when christmas is viewed through Santa's lens. Christmas as experienced in this light becomes oppressive for children, parents, consumers, workers, and the poor. Relatively few people benefit from this kind of christmas fun, but Deegan's (1989a) notion of emancipatory rituals means that all is not lost. The spirit of Christmas and the playfulness of the season can be regained through critical analysis and rejection of rituals that maintain gift-giving as a commodity-exchange or method of social control and rushing through the season without an appreciation for the holiday.

A CHRISTMAS STORY

Santa Claus as a symbolic figure with a major role in the rituals of christmas is considered here as a rite with three major participants: first, American children who function in the role of "believer" in the myth; second, older children and adolescents who stand on the edge of belief and adult cynicism and enjoy gifts given by older people who are usually in a position of authority over them; and, finally, adults who act as Santa's "agents." Christmas in the light of present-day Santa celebrations is a religio-cultural construction that can be both a participatory ritual and a media-constructed ritual. Employing critical dramaturgy, I examine the roles, settings, and patterns of interaction of believers and agents of Santa Claus to reveal the nature of christmas in the United States.

THE AMERICAN SANTA CLAUS

Children in the United States experience Santa Claus as the bringer of toys, goodies, and other gifts, who visits each child's home on 24 December each year. There is an aura of liminality associated with this charming ritual of gift-getting, but this special time is systematically subverted in American society.

Russell W. Belk (1987) claims that the American representation of Santa Claus is not related to older European figures. The hyper-modern Santa Claus does not maintain the religious associations linked to such figures as Santa Lucia and Saint Nicholas. This Santa Claus does not retain the punitive nature of figures such as Sinterklaas, who brings children coal and switches for bad behavior. This Santa Claus, unlike his more ancient predecessors, is "real": Children can touch him at the mall and write to him at the North Pole, and he brings substantial gifts of a manufactured variety. Santa has moved from the sacred point of origin of past Christmas celebrations to the mundane constructions of capitalism, time commodification, and sexism. Santa sells Coca-Cola, and in this light, Santa is a capitalist figure. "Professional Santas," moreover, fill the malls and offer purchasing advice in television commercials. Mrs. Claus remains a shadowy figure, supporting her husband's work. His labor must be completed within the "holiday season" when stores sell merchandise for christmas.

Goffman (1959) provides us with the tools for examining Santa from the frontstage as well as behind the scenes. The front is a dramatic performance conducted for an audience. It consists of the setting as well as the appearance and manner of those who are actors. It is a surface level of action that does not reveal anything more or less than this presentation. For Santa, the front is perhaps best revealed in Clement Moore's 1844 poem "T'was the Night before Christmas." In this classic pose, Santa is a round and jolly man, whose laughter shakes his body like a bowlful of jelly. In my exposition, I go backstage behind this performance and examine Santa's underbelly.

Throughout the remainder of this chapter, I examine Santa as an example of oppression through his reinforcement of core codes, including commodification of time, ageism, and capitalism. To do this, I first establish Santa's American identity.

WHO IS SANTA CLAUS?

Despite the commercial push to make Santa an untarnished symbol, he has been a problematic symbol for over a century. Thus, in 1896 at the University of Nebraska, when it was barely out of its frontier and homestead years, and in an era that is idealized for family holidays, a school teacher, Frances Duncombe, surveyed school-age children to understand Santa Claus from their perspective (Benjamin 1995). She asked older children what they had thought of Santa when they were little children when they were believers of the myth. Their responses ran from "a good spirit in the hearts of people" to "a large man who came around to give presents to good children." The teacher asked the children how they found out who Santa really was. Some children reported that they asked their parents, while others heard clues from parents or saw suspicious activity.

Belk (1987), in a synopsis of the literature on this topic, interprets Santa as an important figure in the core code of ageism (see chapters 9 and 12). Gift-giving from a higher-status person to a lower-status one who is unable to reciprocate with a similar quality gift can be seen as demeaning or hostile. Through the *front* of Santa Claus, acting as an intermediary, the tension of parental authority is reduced.

According to Belk (1987), Santa symbolizes the acquisitive nature of capitalism. Santa's bottomless bag of toys places the emphasis on the gift of consumer goods, especially since Santa is depicted by business. Santa's myth can stand for not only social status, but also moral status in the minds of children. This notion is the most poignant example of the oppressive nature of the Santa Claus phenomenon.

Another question in Duncombe's 1896 survey captured this underside of Santa. She asked older children whether they thought young children should be taught to believe in Santa Claus. A twelve-year-old boy replied:

It is all right for rich people to teach their children to believe in Santa Claus. But not for poor people. Rich people can give their children presents where a poor man cannot. All children will expect presents from Santa Claus. And if they do not receive them they will feel bad. (Benjamin 1995, 193)

Oppression of the child's spirit in this instance is spirit-crushing and grants benefits to those who can afford to provide their children with things, while constraining those who either cannot afford gifts or who feel compelled to go into debt to provide a Santa-like christmas for their children.

Thomas Nast, a political cartoonist during the late-nineteenth and early-twentieth centuries, gave us our picture of what Santa looked like around 1863. It is interesting to note that besides Santa Claus, Nast was noted for such images of "conspicuous consumption" (Veblen 1899) as Boss Tweed and others involved in corrupt machine politics. Belk (1987) notes that there is a striking resemblance between these parodies and the fat Santas drawn by Nast. Perhaps this was no accident. These politicans were known for their wealth, lavish lifestyle, and flagrant use and misuse of bounty at the expense of those with considerably less means. Santa as a media-constructed personage encourages this type of oppressive consumption.

James Frideres (1973) examined the relationship between advertising directed at children and their parents' buying patterns and found that, at christmas time, parents from lower socioeconomic status were most likely to buy items based on their children's desires. This rate of buying based on children's desires at christmas was twice the rate found at other times of the year. Children's wants were related to direct exposure to advertising on television and indirect exposure through friends who had seen commercials. Children make their wish lists for Santa based upon this media hype. Lower-income parents are subjected to the emotions of wanting to please their children at christmas, but the experience of spending more than they can afford becomes oppressive for these adults.

WHERE DOES SANTA LIVE?: THE GLOBALIZATION OF THE AMERICAN SANTA CLAUS

Considerable energy and effort is expended each year to answer letters to Santa Claus. Where do those letters go? How does Santa get them? Daniel Boorstin (1992) has suggested that Americans who are unable to experience reality turn to "pseudo-events" to create illusions or veils for the real world. The more alienated a society, the more likely is that society to create oppressive and repressive fun. Some have termed this process "Disneyfication" (Warren 1994) or the location of such phenomena the "Disney Zone" (Sorkin 1992; see Altman's discussion in chapter 7). Applied to Santa, this means that Americans experience Santa Claus as part of christmas and this replaces the religious holiday that is built on anti-structure. This global phenomenon of American Santa is reflected in the struggle by different nations to claim where Santa lives.

Canada

Canadians claim Santa's home is located in their segment of the Arctic Circle and the waters leading to the North Pole. Santa even has an official Canadian postal code at the North Pole, HOH OHO (Rowley 1993). Each year Toronto holds an annual Santa Claus parade that is beamed into the homes of television viewers around the world, a participatory ritual for a few and a media-constructed ritual for the world. Canada's official policy on letters to Santa is that every child's letter is answered in the child's own language, and retired postal workers answer more than one million letters annually. What does Canada gain from this seemingly liminal approach to Santa? Perhaps Finland provides the answer to this question.

Finland/Lapland versus Norway

In 1927, a Finnish radio announcer informed his listeners that Santa's home had been found along the Finnish-Russian border called Lapland. Through the years, further attempts were made to convince the world that Santa's real home was in Finland. These claims infuriated some Norwegians, however. A group, supported by a Norwegian mayor, even protested against the King of Norway's visiting a site near Finland's state-sponsored Santa Claus Village. Apparently, Norway also considers itself to be the home of Santa Claus.

The Finnish Santa, nonetheless, has traveled around the world spreading the good news that Santa lives in Finland, and he is financed by the Finnish Department of Tourism. National tourism authorities originally believed that Santa tourism would financially benefit the area, but in the early 1990s Finland's Santa Claus Land had severe financial problems. It was disbanded, only to be purchased by a private corporation; it is currently owned by a real estate company. In the new Santa Claus Village, the visitor can find Santa's workshop, a post office, a reindeer enclosure, restaurants, and gift shops. Santa Claus Village is, as Michael Pretes (1995) describes it, a contrived tourist attraction. It has been built and marketed purely to attract visitors: It is a destination. Letters from Santa are no longer sent free of charge from Santa's address book in Finland. Instead, visitors to the village pay 15 marks [approximately $10.00 in 1997] to receive a letter from Santa. Santa is commodified, and visiting him costs a trip to Finland plus fifteen marks. Santa Claus Village is capitalized, commercialized, and commodified. Meanwhile, numerous other villages, towns, and cities around the world also claim to be the home of Santa. Wherever he lives, he brings material consumer goods.

WHAT DOES SANTA BRING?

The rituals surrounding Santa's gift-giving are attractive and alienating, where "fun" is seductive to consumers and profitable to investors

(Deegan 1989a). These rituals are not controlled by ordinary people—either agents or believers—but by manufacturers and the social elite. Thus what Santa brings may be problematic in several ways. Cost is of course an issue, what to buy is also an issue, and finally, we must eventually consider the morality of what we purchase.

The liminal and frontstage dramaturgy of Christmas is presented as an event "for the children" or as "religious." The structural, backstage performance is guided by capitalists who want consumers to "buy buy buy." James Cooper and Kathleen Madigan (1995) report that the holidays are critical for retailers because this period accounts for roughly a third of all annual sales and half of their profits. Clearly this explains why retailers construct a media event capitalizing on the importance of gift-giving. David Haines (1988) notes that Christmas becomes a time of obligation, with a far-from-liminal spirit that is motivated by the "unwanted necessity of buying presents." In this instance christmas is no longer liminal but only another everyday expectation.[2]

Retailers certainly do not want us to focus on behind-the-scenes financial and business quagmires that detract from the idealized meaning of christmas. When Genevieve Buck (1995), a reporter from the *Chicago Tribune*, posed the question: "Was that perfect gift made in a sweatshop?" the capitalist nature of what Santa brings was deftly revealed. What Santa Claus brings costs money, and sweatshops create cheaper items and cost less money than those made by legitimate businesses. The two capital interests come together in a picture of sweatshop christmas gifts that destroys the illusion of a liminal Santa and presents a reality that most retailers would rather the consumer (aka gift-giver/purchaser) not consider.

When one retailer was asked about sweatshop christmas items, he responded:

Life is complicated enough. Don't put an extra burden on them (consumers/Santas). Shopping is part entertainment, part function, but not heavy on drama. Besides there is nothing a customer can do to be assured an item did not come from a sweatshop. (Buck 1995)

Meanwhile, in August 1995 federal authorities busted a California sweatshop operation where typical christmas gifts were made. They found 72 Thai workers in virtual slavery. Workers were paid 72 cents per hour and housing was provided: Workers were locked in and houses were surrounded by barbed wire fences. This is truly the backstage, and retailers may be right: Americans prefer not to know that the bargain they find for their perfect christmas gift is purchased at the expense of another human being's freedom.

This capitalist exploitation of colonial laborers clearly reveals the Santa phenomenon as tyrannical, cruel, and unjust. Again we see the process of oppression and repression in American rituals, where one group has fun while another one suffers. Neither workers nor shoppers gain capital from this, but owners of the means of production profit considerably.

We have already seen that low-income parents are particularly susceptible to their children's wish list at christmas. This pressure to buy may explain why retailers find that the Friday after Thanksgiving is their most profitable day. This day has been termed "Black Friday," but this designation does not have the negative connotations of other black days in recent history (for instance, Black Tuesday and its relationship to the fall of the stock market in 1929). Black Friday refers, instead, to the day that many retailers see their accounting records "in the black." James Cooper and Kathleen Madigan (1994) documented that in 1994 VISA USA reported that credit card charges for this pivotal day hit a record $1.9 million, up 24 percent from the previous year. MasterCard reported its volume up 35 percent in the same period. Plainly, economic forces organize experiences that emerge from what Santa buys.

One interesting way that businesses profit from what Santa brings and at the same time instill a sense of fatherly caretaking (sexism) is through the annual corporate gift, often a gift of a turkey or ham for christmas dinner. Few things can be more symbolic of the sex code than the persistent presence of one's employer as the provider of the holiday feast while other workers are unable to reciprocate. The gift does not come from another person but from a pseudo-person, the corporation. Similarly, christmas parties sponsored by the employer serve as an opportunity for corporate officers rarely seen at other times of the year to pass out the annual bonuses and awards. In this instance we see the symbolic gesture of one who is more powerful giving to those who are not in a position to reciprocate. The employee is often unable to even identify to whom a gift would be sent.

Corporations with an *emphasis on family* may even hire a Santa to pass out gifts to employees' children at the annual event. All these actions maintain the frontstage image of what *christmas is meant to be*, while maintaining backstage the symbolic sex and capital structure of the everyday work setting. It is interesting to note that the modern use of time has made "spending time" on these activities so problematic that many businesses, particularly those in retail sales, have moved their christmas parties to January.

Employees sometimes exchange gifts with one another, often limited to a token of $5 or less. But this apparently liminal gift can require an inordinate investment of time (another way to spend time without pay) to find something *meaningful* and cheap! These gifts may assume the status of obligation, as well. Thus, christmas and Santa involve the core code of hyper-modern time in a complex pattern.

WHEN DOES SANTA COME?: THE HYPER-MODERN
USE OF SANTA'S TIME

Christmas ornaments, artificial trees, toy layaway programs, special wrapping paper, and other reminders of christmas appear on the shelves earlier and earlier each year. They frequently start appearing about the same time that Halloween costumes appear, but in the case of *Star Trek* ornaments, they go on sale in July. These "collectible" consumer products are accompanied by open houses to celebrate the event (see Deegan 1989a, on the *Star Trek* ritual). This extension of the christmas season shows how important the Santa Claus phenomenon is to retailers. Business magazines begin to report on seasonal spending practices in November (Cooper and Madigan 1994, 1995), and by Thanksgiving, the doom-and-gloom projections of "another poor holiday season" for businesses has been declared.

It is also interesting to note that Santa traditionally makes his official entry into town on the big sale day of Black Friday. Friends ask friends, moreover, if they finish their shopping as the holiday approaches (only four weeks away). The clock ticks away and calendar pages fall by the wayside, as time looms heavy for Santa's agents. Meanwhile, Santa will make his trip around the world to good little girls and boys in less than a night. Months of shopping and planning and spending dispensed in one night. Time becomes commodified through the Santa ritual, when parents are constricted by time to have the stage set in the "St. Nick" of time. This emphasis on time, for parents and children, becomes oppressive.

I remember with some dismay a christmas past in which my husband I were busily working away at 2:00 a.m, attempting to complete Santa's work, with the specter of church at 9:00 a.m. and the excited children awake in just a few hours. Time was hanging heavy over our heads when suddenly our child appeared needing to go to the bathroom. Visions of christmas disaster loomed, as we, fatigued by the responsibilities of this joyful season, angrily rushed her off to bed! Our perfect *front stage* performance was about to be destroyed by biological functions and the ever-present clock moving forward. Three long months of preparation, one long night without sleep, and twenty minutes of joy and excitement create a system that is plagued with opportunities for tyranny.

Children may be disappointed with their gifts, and parents may be disappointed with the children's responses to these gifts and may feel alienated. The outcome is that christmas, elaborated by the American Santa Claus, pales in comparison to what adults and children have anticipated for many months. The expanded passage of time has allowed the event to become bigger than life. Deegan (1986a, 790) has suggested similar emotions for recently disabled individuals in their experience of holidays when "Holidays can become times that are dreaded because they fall so short of their idealized emotions." Parents and children cannot be renewed by the flawed christmas event, which has been concocted over the passage of so much time.

CHRISTMAS DAY AND ITS AFTERMATH

As Christmas day approaches and Santa's job is done, the events of christmas seem to settle down. Bureaucracy grinds to a halt as workers go home to celebrate the holidays with family. Stores close early with promises to open bright and early on 26 December with post-christmas sales. On 25 December 1995, the idealized day of liminality, the *Chicago Tribune* headlined an item with this gloomy statement: "Late Rush of Shoppers Can't Cheer Retailers: End-of-Season Sales Bring in Customers, But Markdowns Expected to Wipe Out Profit." The news was that this christmas was a disappointing season in which the last week of the buying season could not make up for previously poor sales and a slow start. The overall industry would eke out only a 1 percent-to-2-percent gain in sales compared to previous years. This was expected to lead to an increase in business bankruptcies and employee layoffs after the holidays. One week later, the same newspaper reported that retail stores had recorded a stagnant christmas, leading to price cuts in post-christmas sales; thus, a bad sign for the job prospects of retail workers ("Another Jolt to Nation's Workers as Economy 'Disconnected'" 1996). Through these stories, consumers and workers alike experience negative emotions from events beyond their ability to control. The consumer feels guilty for the "things" that went unpurchased, chagrin for the neighbor whose job may be lost, and pleasure at the beginning of a new christmas shopping year beginning on 26 December (only 364 days until christmas). Fortunately the consumer is still not weighed down by the knowledge of the working conditions of those who produced the *good deal* (Deegan 1989a, 51–75). Alternatively, the retail worker experiences concern over the purchases he or she made (perhaps utilizing future earnings), fear of what the future may or may not hold; all of this based on the economy of that benevolent bringer of gifts, Santa Claus.

We also cannot forget the families who—despite meals provided by the Salvation Army and gifts purchased by shoppers for poor children, and money collected by Santas standing next to red kettles—experience the crushing disappointment of another year without the gifts they wanted for christmas. For these families, the childlike state of awe associated with the Santa phenomenon always disappoints. The liminal Christmas is not about capitalism, sexism, ageism, or hyper-modern time. Despite Santa's red suit, he is not a communist; he is a capitalist, and those who support him are his agents.

CONCLUSION

Christmas rituals are constructed around the core codes of capitalism, sexim, ageism, and the commodification of time. Santa's agents and believers are coerced by media representations of a liminal Christmas, but instead of this event, they participate in christmas rituals. Santa, perhaps originally modeled around a religious figure, implores believers and agents alike to participate in a flawed holiday that no longer resembles the original intent of the day.

Perhaps the most interesting aspect of this entire ritual is that there is little hostility expressed toward this event. Instead, individuals seem to be alienated from their own experiences of the holiday: buying into, so to speak, the entire phenomenon. Instead of the joy of a liminal experience, agents and believers are connected to events through the demands and obligations of Santa's season. Childlike awe is replaced with mandates on time and financial resources. The rule of reciprocation replaces the spirit of gifting. In this light, christmas is hollow and flawed. It mimics the shell of the holiday Christmas. When the package is torn open on christmas day, Christmas is not to be found.

Deegan (1989a) suggests that all is not lost. She proposes that we can avoid these old ways of doing ritual through critical analysis. We must engage in emancipatory rituals and celebrations and return to a ritual life that is playful. We, in the instance of Christmas, must regain our sense of childlike wonder, removing the focus on money and time racing forward. The holiday must be taken out of the hands of business and returned to the control of everyday people. In this way the rituals of Christmas can "capture our hearts and emotions" (Deegan 1989a, 167). In this playful approach we shall give gifts with generosity, share with those around us in everyday life, party with those with whom we celebrate, and move through the holiday rituals without a sense of commodified time. In reinventing the season, the frontstage and backstage will disappear as superficial performances with and for others. The other joins the self in a time of celebration and renewal. If we enjoy Christmas, then the oppressive nature of a business-constructed holiday is replaced with a holiday of fantasy and play for all!

NOTES

1. The word "christmas" is spelled with a lowercase letter to indicate the oppressive and repressive characteristics associated with this holiday, especially Santa Claus. This differentiates it from the Christian ritual celebration, spelled with a capital "C."

2. Deegan (1986a) describes holidays that fall short of their liminal meaning and emotions as particularly stressful for the recently physically disabled.

V

American Rituals and the Sacred in Hyper-Modern Society

9

American Ritual
and American Gods

Anthony J. Blasi

It is a "cute" commonplace of long standing for someone to describe religion in America as a weekend option that competes with more professedly
leisure-time activities. The implications of that description are that the
Sabbath has been transformed by the secular ethic into "weekend" and
that religion has sufficiently lost its significance so that it is now counted
among such weekend trivia as televised spectator sports, fishing, and
recreational shopping. According to one major observer, Thomas Luckmann (1967), religion *per se* is an inevitable aspect of life, a serious and
self-transcending dimension of everyday consciousness, and that it is
churches that are optional recreations. Be that as it may, religion by its
very nature proposes claims to transcendence; it presents a perspective
that is tangential to, rather than derivative of, this-worldly life. It therefore shares space, as it were, with other activities that would be departures from the workaday world; it is one of several pursuits found in
Americans' "off times."

Not all ritual events are equivalent alternatives; some succeed in oc-
casioning the formation of true departures from wider oppressive structures and some do not. Those that succeed, following Deegan's (1989a)
terminology, are "play" and those that do not are "fun." Since religious
phenomena are quite diverse, it should come as no surprise that sometimes they resemble play and sometimes fun. Identifying which religious
phenomena are which can be an interesting and informative endeavor,
but it is more important to see why and how religion has come to be, at

one and the same time, implicated in and dissociated from the wider oppressive structures of American society. So the first step in the present analysis involves a survey of institutions in the American setting and a characterization of the place of religion among them.

MACRO AND MICRO INSTITUTIONS AND THEIR ORGANIZATIONS

The major institutions in the United States may be divided between the "macro" type, whose highly placed executives may cross institutional lines and assume leadership roles in organizations in institutional sectors other than those in which they first assumed executive responsibility, and the "micro" type. C. Wright Mills (1956) identified three institutions as what are termed here "macro institutions"—big military, big business, and the executive branch of the federal government. The suggestion is that high-ranking military officers can leave the armed services organizations and assume executive responsibilities in major corporations, and that high-ranking business executives can leave the private sector and assume executive responsibilities in federal departments. This horizontal mobility at the top of the social pyramid constitutes something of a circulation of elites. In contrast, leaders of organizations in the micro institutions—principally the family, local education, and religion—cannot expect reasonably to transfer from one sector to another: to assume leadership positions either in a macro institution or in one of the other micro types. Hence, a family head cannot expect to become an Air Force general on the grounds of family leadership experience, or even assume leadership in another micro institution, for example, as a school principal or church official, on such grounds.[1] The macro institutions are linked tightly to one another, while the micro institutions are linked, at best, loosely.

The macro institutions, of course, are asymmetrically related to the micro ones. When major corporations raise prices, relocate plants, or lay off large numbers of employees, the impact is wrought upon families, schools, and churches; alternatively, however, the typical family, school, or congregation does not affect such a corporation in any significant way. Similarly, actions by the military or by the federal executive may bring about war or peace, military-base relocations, economic growth or stagnation—each having a significant impact on the micro organizations, without any comparable influence from the micro institutions creating significant events that would impinge upon the macro institutions' organizations (Blasi 1994). In this context, religion, embodied in organizations of a micro-institutional form, is subject to contingencies that are set in motion from the major institutional sector but that is unable to set a religious agenda for them in any significant way.[2]

Religion as Fun

By way of a first thesis, we can argue that generic, structural oppression in a free society takes the form, in part, of the asymmetrical relationship between the interconnected major institutions on the one hand and the loosely connected micro types on the other. As applied to off time, we would find this structural phenomenon exemplified by the contamination of what would otherwise be spontaneous and improvisational play in micro-institutional settings. "Contamination" is a value-loaded term that implies that something religious is being rendered less religious or even useless by adding features from some foreign element. For purposes of discussion, let us set aside the value that might be placed on uncontaminated off time so that we can see in what respect a foreign element enters into it and renders it "fun time."

Careerism

In our first example, we can observe that major players in the organizations of the macro institutions (hereafter macro organizations) live out careers that consist of pre-entry patterns of preferred socialization, entry points, routine promotions, events that catch the notice of "sponsors" higher up still in the organization, and nonroutine promotions into leadership positions. The *career*, in this sense, consists of a sequence of occasions in which ambitious organizational climbers can respond to any propensities they may have for individualistic opportunism. A calculating mentality, coupled with a feigned undeliberate mode of coming to superiors' attention in a positive light, pervades the wide-awake consciousness and after a while pervades as well the "second nature" of the fast-track executive. Engaging in strategic recreation so as to make organizational contacts and prove one's loyalty to the organization provides a common occasion of fun for such fast trackers (Kanter 1977). Much as executives disguise self-advancement for productivity, they also disguise it as recreation.

Careerism contaminates religion most evidently in the organizational structures of churches and other religious entities that resemble corporate, military, and governmental bureaucracies (see chapter 1 for a discussion of Deegan's core code of bureaucracy). One thinks of church boards that resemble corporation boards, religious orders that resemble military organizations, and Vatican City's parallels to other national governmental apparatus. However, this is not what needs to be brought to attention here; rather, it is a matter of clericalism. In clericalism, religious specialists set about performing as work lines of conduct that correspond to nonspecialists' nonwork. Sexism enters here; some would have the clergy be all-male because work has been stereotypically male. The division between clergy and laity, a division of *labor*, may or may not be explained in terms of some ideological rationale, but either way it commodifies the workings of the soul. The nonspecialist fashions an attentiveness to the doings of the cleric, whereby the cleric succeeds in eliciting a second-hand religiosity in the nonspecialist. Full authenticity of religious functions becomes defined in terms of the clergy's deeds rather than the laity's initiatives.

Entrepreneurialism

Life in macro institutions brings entrepreneurialism to the fore. In contrast to small business, where entrepreneurship involves making a going concern out of a small entity (which has its own counterpart in religion), entrepreneurialism in macro-institutional settings involves making arrangements for *others* to undertake complex tasks. The entrepreneurs propose restructuring plans, advocate new strategies, associate their names with faddish managerial techniques—do everything but attend to the substance of the enterprise. They operate in a world of events that parallel the production units with something of an overlay of conferences, seminars, and workshops—each with a cryptic name that includes a "hook" word such as "encounter," "growth," "goals," and "objective."

In religious settings, this particular kind of entrepreneurship involves programs that travel from congregation to congregation. Hierarchical administrators, where they exist (as in "connectional" churches), may find one or more such programs appealing and may promote them among the local churches. In less hierarchical religions, clergy tend to come upon these programs through their own social networks, either of other clergy or of corporate executives whom they happen to know. The church becomes another "unit" over which the entrepreneurial, parallel world of training sessions comes to be spread. What is significant about entrepreneurship is that every increment of initiative that is structured into such programs represents that much less space for initiative left to the nonspecialists; congregational or parish "involvement" becomes a matter of fitting into scripted roles, functions, steps, phases, and so on.

Macro Secular Ethos

The macro organizations generate a great deal of compulsiveness in their host societies. The present concern is not so much the drivenness of the careerist's psychology but the expectation that everything has a relevant policy statement that is applicable in some compulsory way. The inhabitant of such entities looks for *the* right way of doing things, *the* right things to do, and *the* assignment of particular functions to different people. Standardization and a division of labor, reflecting an authoritative structure, lead to a diffuse ethos of hyper-normativity no less ineluctable than a teenage dress code. The ethos holds that one only does what one is assigned to do, and that what one does should follow one of a limited sampler of behavioral paradigms.

The degree to which the religious scene is pervaded by this macro secular ethos can be seen, first, by the limited scope of what are considered to be proper religions. The person who dabbles with a religion that is "out of class"—a poor or working-class person in a rich-person's denomination, a prosperous person in a lower-class sect, or any person in a marginal or exotic cult—soon encounters the limits of the list of approved spiritual pursuits. Beyond that, there is the propensity of religions' moral sensitivities to become normative codes. For reasons of respectability, conventional taboos become lists of sins, while little comparable emphasis is placed on proactive steps people might take to make the world more just, sane, or wise. Ethical sensitivities are left to be inert while systems of congregational and ecclesiastical approval and disapproval reinforce standardized codes of moral proscriptions.

In keeping with the organizational pattern in the macro-institutional sector, where every eventuality needs to have a policy statement in place, contaminated religion treats traditional scriptures—no matter how poetic, allegorical, or inspirational they may be—as organizational policy handbooks. Alternatively, they may codify their procedures and ethics in systems of law—depending on whether they are fundamentalist or hierarchical in nature. The former take their scriptures literally, while the latter use scriptures to legitimate codes of ecclesiastical norms. In either instance, the intent is to banish ambiguity, to leave no question open. This thoroughly disempowers nonexecutive individuals since it persuades them to abdicate moral responsibility for decision making, much as macro organizations disempower line staff. In fact, one could see contaminated religion as a subsystem that socializes people in their innermost souls so that they could become or continue to be properly disposed functionaries at the lower levels in the organization charts of the macro organizations.

RELIGION AS PLAY

The fact that religions appeal to the transcendent leaves open the logical potential of religiously minded persons becoming immune to the this-worldly claims of both macro and micro organizations. Because of the centrality of macro organizations and the only loosely connected pattern among the micro organizations, immunity to the claims of the former has greater and more difficult implications for the lines of conduct of the individual. In this potential play, transcendentally inspired immunity is implicitly an inoculation against macro-organizational contamination. Such an inoculation derives from subcultural contents of two kinds: little traditions and great (terms often used by Robert Redfield; see Redfield 1962, 57). Little traditions tend to be folkish and magical in nature, often associated with nonrational expressiveness (for example, speaking in tongues) and unofficial or alternative varieties of science and medicine (for example, belief in auras and utilization of non-medical healing practices). Great traditions tend to involve their adherents in intellectual traditions of theology and moral reasoning that may entail a mastery of archaic languages, millennia of philosophical or legal reasoning, or well–worked-out systems of moral decision making and counsel. In both the little and the great traditions, the adepts engage in lines of conduct and expand along dimensions of consciousness that are repressed in macro-organizational contexts or in contexts in the micro-institutional sector that are contaminated by a macro ethos of some kind.

Playful Religion as Nonbureaucratic

One feature of playful religion is its nonoccupational, noncareerist modality. Religious entities for the laity at least are voluntary organizations, and they usually have smaller entities within them—choirs, charities, study groups—that are also voluntary. Music, in particular, occasions a participatory religious expressionism that contrasts with not only the workaday structures of corporate society, but also with the commodified, nonparticipatory "media" versions of music (see Lincoln and Mamiya 1990, 346–81). The group-level religious involvement has a counterpart at the individual level, "devotionalism," that may consist of a meditative reading of a traditional text, private prayer practices, or even keeping a journal of the soul in the manner of the late United Nations secretary general Dag Hammarskjold. It is informative to contrast both the group and the individual level of nonoccupational pursuits of religious play with some superficially similar activities in quite different contexts. In the case of industry-generated market music, not only is the productive activity work for the recording artists, but it is promoted as nonserious diversion, the stuff of fads that fuel an ever-changing (and hence ever market re-creating) recorded music scene. Religious musical participation, however, plays upon the serious side of life, emotionally exploring themes rather than diverting attention; in this respect, it resembles tragic opera more than a Top Ten hit list. Moreover, it is comprised of a blend of contemporary creations and traditional favorites, thereby bridging past and present rather than hyping a sale of the moment. Individual daydreaming at the work place is also a diversion, usually from inherently uninteresting tasks. It may be justified as rest from mental labor or from routine, or it may even be experienced with an accompaniment of guilt feelings over wasted time. Devotional activity is experienced quite differently—as getting to the heart of matters rather than as a diversion, and as constituting important and even precious time.

Playful Religion and Nonmodern Time

Religious play embodies a continuity with the past as a *process* of tradition rather than as a traditional *content*. Processes of tradition resemble education as intellectual empowerment (versus education as rote memorization or social control). One who is intellectually empowered grasps a meaning from the past, whether the logic of a mathematical procedure or the sense of a poem, *not* as an external object but as an internal thought or discovery. We sometimes call this the "aha experience," wherein we discover the utter simplicity of the most difficult truths or insights. A simple insight from the past reaches us in a present recognition. Religious tradition as process similarly enlivens old symbols with present experience, revealing the simple limitedness of human consciousness in the very act of expanding its awareness of the transcendent. This seemingly has little to do with the "all questions are closed" nature of fun religion.

Playful Religion as Open to Rules and Meaning

A common sign of playful religion is its parable morality. A parable challenges people, often with a narrative that describes a break with some convention. The hearers or readers are confronted with a moral logic that implies that some line of action that would usually be condemned or at least questioned as paradoxical embodies a defensible value stance. The hearer or reader is given no final answer but is left to draw inferences for principled action. No "moral policy" is set; instead, one decides on matters on the basis of spontaneous but certainly not willful responses. Rather than be a prisoner of one's own wants—as one is in the ideal, commercial economy wherein professional purveyors of hype seek to arouse a variety of urges to buy gratifying experiences—one is led to appreciate a moral logic that would occasion free responses to the dramas of social life.

CONCLUSION: THEORETICAL PROSPECT

The consideration of religion as off time leads toward the conceptual expansion of *fun* and *play*. The failure of fun to achieve liminality can be associated with the neo-Marxian theme of the commodification of culture, while the potential of play to approach the liminal can be associated with *la vie serieuse*. Fun can be seen as an unwitting reception of a prepackaged cosmos, while play can be seen as a witful employment of heritages for purposes of cosmos construction. Modalities of participation in fun can be seen as diversions, while those of participation in play can be seen as exercises of sensitization. Moral conformity hyped by fun can be contrasted to moral decision making. Not only religion, but *mythos* understood more broadly can be seen as an activizing element in collective life, a regenerative undercurrent in the protest against suffering, in the sigh, in the popular logic, and in the encyclopedic compendium of oppressed folk (Marx 1967, 250). The fate of religious times in America and elsewhere is a serious matter with pervasive moral implications.

NOTES

1. Family and school connections may be used, however, by someone already having an elite status; this is a simple consequence of the self-selection of the power elite with their dependents into a semi-segregated life space.

2. This is not for lack of trying; the "new Christian right" endeavored to further a legislative agenda by means of a political alliance with economic conservatives, only to find its own agenda largely ignored by the economic conservatives it helped elect.

10

A Sacred Myth in Secular Packaging: Gillan's Journey Through the Witch World

Mary Jo Deegan

The Witch World is a gripping fantasy of the mythic struggles between the gods of another planet. It emerges from the imagination of Andre Norton, a great American storyteller whose role parallels that of story-tellers in traditional societies. She is living, of course, in a hyper-modern society (Giddens 1990): Her stories are written and not oral; and are shared by some, but not all, people. She is, moreover, not telling sacred myths of a people; she creates an international audience (Goffman 1959) that consists of millions of readers of her "popular" myths. Norton draws on a rich multicultural vision culled from history, anthropology, and folk-lore, and our primordial interest in adventure, fear, and courage. Her Witch World is, paradoxically, a sacred myth in secular packaging: a fan-tasy series emerging from American popular culture but linked to sacred dramas and international dreams.

Although Norton has published over 125 novels (see Schlobin and Harrison 1995), few scholars have studied her corpus despite her popu-larity, complex thought, and intellectual significance (Schlobin is a par-ticularly notable exception, see 1993, 1994; Yoke 1991). The Witch World series alone includes over 30 books, several anthologies, and many authors in addition to Norton.

At least one reason Norton's work is often overlooked is that her books defy categorization as either "high-brow" or "low-brow" literature. What-ever category of class and taste they fit, they are popular: 10 million cop-ies of Witch World books had been sold worldwide by 1987 (information from book jacket rear flap), and many more millions have been sold since then. They are on the shelves of hundreds of public libraries as well. Norton's books tap into scholarly writings and primitive images of the bestial in animal and human forms. Thus, darkness, light, death, life, good, evil, physical disability, exhaustion, and renewal are integral components in her tales of adventure and trial (Turner 1967).

Norton's "heroes," moreover, are often female, intelligent, independent, and physically enduring. Despite the recent growth in feminist scholarship in science fiction, Norton remains "betwixt and between" feminists, scholars, genre fiction, and cultural myths. Victor Turner calls this "betwixt and between" status "liminal." This liminality is "antistructural" or different from the everyday, profane structure (Turner 1969, 1974). Thus, Norton's tales are "betwixt and between" everyday life and the sacred, and she shares this shadowy status in the world of "serious" analysis. In addition, her books are often ambiguously labeled "juvenile" literature, yet they fascinate people of all ages. Even her name is gendered "male" while she is a woman.

Here I employ "critical dramaturgy," a contemporary offshoot of early feminist pragmatism to analyze Norton's American ritual dramas (Deegan 1989a, 1996b, 1997). I analyze her "formula"—or conventional system for structuring cultural products (Cawelti 1969, 386–88)—as similar to that of Frank L. Baum. His wonderful Oz series, based on a unique American vision, had a major adventurous role for female protagonists, especially Dorothy and other little girls. Baum's formula employed antistructural rules to anchor experience, emotions, and ideas (Deegan 1989a, 92; his formula is the opposite of the patriarchal Freudian formula, see Deegan 1989a, 159–67). It is an emancipatory formula because:

Baum's conception of humans evolves from a loving view. Although humans are often frail and prone to error, they have kind hearts and a will to do good. They can exhibit courage, good humor, and a group consciousness that transcends immediate perils. Both men and women are capable of much goodness, but it is little girls who epitomize it. . . . Both good and evil exist, and each struggles for primacy. Good is intrinsically more powerful, but individuals must choose to enact it or evil will triumph. (Deegan 1989a, 130)

Baum's world is inhabited by good and wicked witches, but humans can threaten evil beings because of the power of human goodness (Deegan 1989a, 131). This American myth was originally written in the 1900s and 1910s in Chicago, at the very time and place that feminist pragmatism was emerging in the work and writings of Jane Addams, George Herbert Mead, and John Dewey (Deegan 1988a, 1997).

This congruence in the visions of Norton and Baum is not accidental. Norton is a fan of Baum and was inspired by his writings, as a child. She notes: "The Oz books were my passionate like when I was young, they are still on my shelves and I read one or another over again every once in a while. To my mind they are the only true American fairy tales" (Norton to author, 14 February 1995, 1–2).

Critical dramaturgy allows us to analyze the "ritual process" experienced by Gillan, the heroine on a journey of social and self-discovery in *The Year of the Unicorn*, a Witch World saga. I analyze Norton's fantasies as the "data" or "myth" in a way that is similar to Victor Turner's work on African people and on sacred pilgrimages (1969, 1971, Turner and Turner 1978), but neither Norton nor I claim to be studying a world religion or culture as Turner does (Deegan 1995b). The Witch World is betwixt and between such serious stuff. I am talking about the transformative power of a "good story" to put our daily cares behind us while we vicariously experience a journey to another time and place. Norton emerges from a modern, written tradition about people with special gifts and destinies. In this arena, the word is sacred.

As one witch in a Norton saga explains to another:

Most people never realize that words are important, that they matter, that to say a thing is to give it at least a shadow of existence—and to name it truly is to give it life. You hear, you listen, and you remember, and that is a rare gift. Without it, you would never understand magic. (Bradley, May, and Norton 1990, 361)

These witches and Norton's fans share this fascination with words and miracles.

THE JOURNEY IN *THE YEAR OF THE UNICORN*

The Year of the Unicorn (Norton 1965a) takes place in the "Witch World," and all the basic characteristics of this land are established in the first novel in the series, *Witch World* (Norton 1963). Interdimensional gates allow entry into the Witch World from other worlds, and human beings from Earth occasionally enter it. The most powerful society on the planet, Estcarp, is governed by the Council of Witches. This matriarchy is hated and feared by the more patriarchal "nations" that surround it. Thus, Karsten to the South and Alizon to the North are aiding an alien species, the Kolder, to attack Estcarp in a war that is a major drama in several books in the series.

There are many different types of beings besides "normal humans": for example, gryphons, witches, intelligent "horses" and "lizards," gods and goddesses. The "magical" forces are concentrated in two areas on the planet: Escore and the Waste. Many of the adventures that confront Gillan, the heroine, and Herrel, her mysterious and strange husband, are unique to this Witch World saga, while many other aspects are common to most Witch World stories. Thus the Were-Riders, men who can assume animal forms in a manner similar to legendary werewolves, are found in a number of Witch World books, but their history and functioning are summarized only briefly there, while they are essential to this story. The land they traverse, the Waste, is central to all the Witch World sagas on the Western Continent.

All action in the Witch World is liminal: The Witch World is clearly anti-structural and this different world is entered through gates. In *Horn Crown* (Norton 1981), for example, the entering people are escaping a dying world. They randomly chose to enter an unknown land because the known one is so dreadful. Despite this ever-present liminality of the planet, there is usually an important transition between the profane, "everyday" Witch World and another, more magical and unstable, sacred world with different spaces and rules. Norton, therefore, "plays" with anti-structure and liminality in all her Witch World novels (Deegan 1989a). She does this through "layering or compounding liminality" as a dramatic device. (This concept is similar to Goffman's concept of "keying" or "re-keying frames" [1974].)

This layering of liminality occurs with the protagonists, too. They are usually "multi-liminal"—or experience several "marginal" statuses simultaneously (Deegan in press). Thus they are often poor, homeless, alone, physically weak or challenged, socially or racially ambiguous, and young. They are usually unskilled in magic, an essential skill in the Witch World, and in the ways of survival. Norton's use of multiple liminality usually opens her story with a person in the midst of deep, complex dilemmas and seeking answers to different troubles.

THE CAST AND NARRATIVE

Gillan is the protagonist and narrator of *The Year of the Unicorn*, and she exhibits this "multi-liminality." She is an orphan without a traditional family or home. She is raised in Abbey Norstead, a type of convent that would be found in medieval Europe. This abbey is a gender-segregated "sacred space" to the women who live there, but the unhappy Gillan finds it a narrow, profane world where she is neither free nor at home. Gillan is young, about 20 years old, and without any significant social status at the start of her journey. Rather than continue her cheerless and dreary life, she elects to become a bride of a Were-Rider, a member of an efficient but strange group of men from the magical and threatening land, the Waste.

These men ride the Waste because they, too, are homeless. They are even more liminal than Gillan who is wholly human. The Were-Riders are part human and part beast. They are kin to those mythical monsters—werewolves—who are the subject of countless horror movies and nightmares in our world. The Were-Riders take on the animal bodies and some of the consciousness of the beasts they display on their helms and shields. They are particularly prone to this transformation during the phases of the full moon. Humans, like Gillan, do not know this hidden facet of the Were-Riders, but people are uneasy in their presence and sense something is amiss.

The shape-changers, or Were-Riders, have fought recently on the side of the humans from High Hallack in a war against the Hounds of Alizon. In an interesting juxtaposition, the "Hounds" are "real" humans but act like beasts, while the Were-Riders are bestial but act like humans. The Hounds, moroever, are accompanied by vicious, dog-like animals who murder on command. The Hounds are allied with the Kolder, an enemy that uses weapons from some other, unnamed world. These weapons are similar to armaments—such as tanks, computerized missiles, and rocket throwers—that are found in our world.

The strange Were-Riders are mercenaries who only enter the war to win a prize for themselves. If High Hallack wins the war, the Were-Riders demand 13 brides, maidens between the ages of 18 and 20, in exchange for their services. They promise to leave High Hallack and return to their weird, unknown place in the Waste. This "Great Bargain" was the product of fear and desperation in High Hallack, so the men who struck the deal are reluctant to fulfill their obligations after the war and deliver "their" women. The Were-Riders exact their price, nonetheless, on the first day of the new year: the year of the unicorn. The novel recounts many adventures that occur during that year.

Gillan is not beautiful nor does she "belong" to any family, so she is not "traded" by the men. One terrified young woman is offered as a sacrifice, but Gillan disguises herself and takes her place as one of the chosen maids. At this time, Gillan is unaware of the nature and depth of her own magical powers or the unusual nature of her husband-to-be. She is fleeing a bleak future in the abbey on the chance that even a mysterious, dangerous future is an improvement.

Gillan is discovered as a "false" maiden after it is too late to return to the abbey. She soon compounds her outsider status by selecting Herrel, the Wronghanded, as her husband. He has a low standing with the Were-Riders at the start of the novel, but it apparently improves as he learns to accept himself and to love Gillan. He inadvertently reveals his "animal" persona to Gillan, but to his surprise, he does not lose her love. Thus Gillan and Herrel are both multi-liminal. They are young adults making a *rite de passage* into adulthood; they are newlyweds making a *rite de passage* between being single and married; and they are both untried and without a social status.

Part of their social journey involves conflicts with Halse, the Strongarmed. He is Herrel's enemy and was not claimed as a husband by a young maid. Halse is arrogant, physically strong, a powerful sorcerer, and a leader among the Were-Riders. He is an "insider" who becomes an outsider, however, due to his failure to attract a bride. He despises and envies Herrel, who has a growing self-possession and respect within the Were-Riders because of his new bride. Herrel has another enemy, Hyron, the Captain of the Were-Riders. He is not as overt an enemy as Halse, but he only grudgingly includes Herrel within the group. Hyron appears to enforce the rules of the Were-Riders, but he is frustrated by the laws and the demands for justice advanced by Gillan and Herrel. Gillan's previously unsuspected and, therefore, untrained magical powers disturb the tenuous balance of power between gods and their servants in the strange and twisted landscape. Unlike all the other brides, she has her own vision of herself, independent of her husband.

In addition to Herrel, Gillan befriends Kildas, another bride of the Were-Riders, who is slightly more aware and kind to Gillan than are the other brides. Generally, the brides are a passive, mindless group who are easily controlled by the Were-Riders who employ magic to manage them. Gillan is an outsider to this group of women from High Hallack. She serves as a feminist model who rejects traditional roles and actions for women.

A RITUAL ANALYSIS

In some ways, *The Year of the Unicorn* is a romance that takes place in a medieval tale of good against evil. Gillan's unfolding discovery of her strengths as a person with magical powers, perhaps like a witch's, is a story of interpersonal growth. It follows numerous changes: in maturity, marital status, knowledge, observation, judgment, wisdom, and courage. The "moral" of the story is that love, faith, and hope can overcome seemingly impossible odds. This is an optimistic story where good triumphs over evil and where girl meets boy and falls in love. It is not a simplistic story, but it echoes mythic legends and folktales.

The Year of the Unicorn has a powerful ending. The crafty evil of Halse and his thugish followers is revealed in a battle between good and evil. Gillan dies and Herrel, who had betrayed her in a physical, animal attack beyond his human control, brings her back from the land of the dead. This is the imaginative drama one expects in a "good read," but Norton pushes beyond formulaic endings. The final battle shows the collusion of Hyron, the leader of the Were-Riders, who consistently supported evil in order to rid himself of these innocent but disliked scapegoats. Gillan and Herrel fight back against the society's corruption and reject the entire group as one permeated with hatred, not only for them, but for anything good.

This is not merely a "romantic" ending for a couple in love who can conquer the world alone. It is a moral decision requiring courage and hope.

In the final lines of the story, Herrel reveals that Hyron is actually his father as well as the clan leader, and Hyron's betrayal of his son is an even greater crime than the reader had known. When Gillan and Herrel end their journey, they have forged a new bond, group, and conscience. They do not end in a traditional rite of incorporation (Van Gennep 1960) into their original society; they start a new journey into the unknown after rejecting their society.

This book examines some of the greatest themes of human storytelling: betrayal by the clan, the family, and one's mate. Death, love, magic, and friendship are also explored. The heroine is an independent woman with few material or social resources, and her adventures are far different from male heroes such as Tarzan, Rambo, or Conan.

Despite this female model, Norton employs many of the formulas used in traditional male "adventure" stories. Thus, Gillan is involved in a series of "dirty tricks" that she barely survives, in a manner that echoes the life of Indiana Jones or Flash Gordon. Norton makes these adventures more than devices to confound her readers, however. Her heroine continually avoids the traps set before her by learning more about herself and her enemies. She draws on physical and mental strengths. She reflects on past experiences and chooses to act with moral goodness (see a similar model of self and reflexivity in Mead 1934). She ultimately chooses intimacy without surrendering her humanity. Male heroes rarely select intimate partners, but are involved in endless endings and beginnings of intimacy (see my analysis of Captain Kirk's endless romances in *Star Trek* [Deegan 1989a]).

This book and others in the Witch World series can be read by juvenile readers as wholesome "yarns." This superficial reading is in itself enjoyable, but it is only the simplest interpretation of a complex story. This type of reading has been a barrier to Norton's acceptance as a serious writer of cultural myths. Another barrier is that Norton's heroines do not make "politically correct" feminist decisions in their struggles to face their problems.

For example, one of the "serious" critiques of women's lives in this book arises from the constrictive, unexciting life that Gillan, an orphan, endures within a women's abbey. This women-only society is not idealized. Anything, including an arranged marriage to pay a war debt, is better than her dreary future as a charity case. This is a radical critique of women's limited choices: A rational decision to marry even a potentially inhuman, male-like being is empowering for impoverished women in a patriarchal society even in a woman-only space such as the abbey. After Gillan chooses a mate, moreover, she is not misled by the Were-Riders' illusions as are the other women. Where they see flowers, enjoy sumptuous beds, and dine on gourmet wines and food, Gillan sees a sere wilderness, crude lodging, and minimal rations. Gillan makes her choices without "a cloak-spell" clouding her judgment, and this infuri-ates the "men" who literally "take" brides without their full consent.

The men who oppose Gillan's independence, led by Halse, escalate their attacks against her. She is separated into two beings: One has her physical appearance and is controlled by the evil magic of the men, the other exists as a shadow with dwindling physical strength but with her own mind and soul. The men in the group enjoy her mindless, soulless "fetch" while her "true spirit" endures adventure after adventure. The duality between women's appearance and their spirit is explicit. The vic-tory of reuniting them emerges from the superior strength of Gillan's new being, which is stronger than the magic of men.

Men can be villains who prevent Gillan's completion and control of her journey. For example, the "true" Gillan is almost raped and murdered by a roving band of the Hounds of Alizon, who lost the recent war. Then, af-ter using magic to kill these marauders, she encounters physical and mental barriers protecting the homeland of the Were-Riders. Next, "That Which Runs the Ridges," a foul thing that is part animal and part evil spirit, attacks her during the night after she is exhausted in every mean-ing of the word. As Gillan explains: "Fear can kill, and I had never met such fear as this before. For this did not lurk in any dream, but in the world I had always believed to be sane and understandable" (Norton 1965a, 138).

Again, Gillan defeats a monstrous enemy, only to be confronted by fur-ther trials and magic. There is a progression in these tests from initially physical, external battles to increasingly subjective, internal struggles. Although Norton does not dichotomize physical and mental strengths, she does portray faith and moral character as more important facets of being human than physical stamina and muscles.

The Witch World draws on images similar to those of prehistoric socie-ties such as Stonehenge, the Arthurian legends, and folktales of magical beings and woods. She combines these great, universal stories with popular techniques employed in the genres of adventure, romance, and juvenile literature.

COMPARING THE NORTON AND BAUM FORMULAS

Dorothy's adventures in Oz and Gillan's adventures in the Waste share a number of similarities. Norton's adventures and protagonists, however, are older, and confront sexuality, death, family betrayal, social corruption, and the cosmos. The scale of the myths are grander in Norton than in Baum and more critical. Her Witch World formula can be sum-marized in this way:

Although humans are often frail and prone to error, they can develop a will to do good. They have responsibility for their actions because they make choices, often complex and difficult ones. They can exhibit courage, loyalty, and a group consciousness that transcends immediate perils. Both men and women are capable of goodness, but women are often the caretakers of magic. Both good and evil exist, and each struggles for primacy. Good is intrinsically more powerful, but individuals must choose to enact it or evil will triumph.

The Norton formula is mythic in scale while remaining a "popular" story in "genre fiction." One reason this is not the "great literature" of a people is that she alone creates it in her intergalactic imagination, although she draws on primordial symbols, archetypes, and stories from various cultures and eras to tap the "collective consciousness" (Durkheim 1915; Norton 1975).

These symbols and myths are often compatible with tales of goddesses, female icons, and matriarchal societies. Norton has developed a "feminist pragmatist formula" that is both rooted in American values and simultaneously not well understood in the feminist or women's studies' literature. This formula has a tradition that emerges from American liberal values and our belief in a rational public that is combined with a cooperative, nurturing, and liberating model of the self, the other, and the community. Feminist pragmatism emphasizes education and democracy as significant mechanisms to organize and improve society (Deegan 1995a, 1997; Deegan and Hill 1987, 1989).

Feminist pragmatism challenges our contemporary society, which is built on patriarchal myths, gods, and icons. Norton seriously challenges and undermines patriarchal rules and meanings, but she does so through "entertainment" and liberal American myths such as those revealed in Baum's fairy tales of Oz. Norton's sacred ritual in secular packaging has flourished and grown as a liminal story of resistance.

IMPACT OF THE NORTON FORMULA ON WOMEN'S LITERATURE AND ISSUES

Norton's Witch World formula is highly innovative: It radically challenges the patriarchal worldview that permeates science fiction. It has inspired other writers, especially women, to employ similar formulas and to develop variations on it. Norton has changed the landscape of writing science fiction and fantasy, and this accomplishment was recognized by her peers when she was awarded the Gandalf in 1977 and named "Grand Master" in 1983 (Deegan 1996).

The power and success of the Norton formula is acknowledged publicly and generously by many science-fiction authors in other ways, too. In fact, the number of famous, "serious" science-fiction writers inspired by Andre Norton is staggering. For example, Anne McCaffrey and C. J.

Cherryh have each dedicated a book to Norton. Marion Zimmer Bradley, Tanith Lee, Judith Tarr, and Poul Anderson are only a few notable authors who acknowledge Norton's influence on their work and lives (see more tributes in the anthology edited by Susan Shwartz 1985). There are other short story collections inspired by the series; see Norton's anthologies on *Tales of the Witch World* (1987, 1989, 1990). Many of these authors are the subject of scholarly analyses, but these scholars—unlike the authors they study—rarely acknowledge Norton's influence.

In other words, Norton is an acknowledged mentor or "moonsinger" (a nickname for Norton, who uses this figure in one series; see Deegan 1996) for writers, but scholars have been unable or unwilling to understand how her intellectual leadership emerged. One explanation is offered here: The Norton formula radically changed the relationship between men and women depicted in science fiction and fantasy writing, but most scholars do not understand the depth of her ideas and influence. Science-fiction authors influenced by Norton acknowledge her leadership, but some scholars attribute these innovations to Norton's followers and not to Norton. Another explanation of Norton's scholarly neglect is that Norton's scholarship is often in the social sciences and history, while many scholars of genre fiction are trained in English and the study of literature.

Authors, particularly female ones, who create sociologically informed fiction are systematically misunderstood (Deegan 1997; Hill 1987; 1989). Norton's feminism, moreover, does not fit the ideals elaborated by Marxist feminists, cultural feminists, or popular liberal feminists. She breaks the bounds of hyper-modern feminism in a mythical world.

Norton's influence is beyond the formulaic and emerges from the intersection between the text and the reader's imagination. The noted science-fiction author Joan D. Vinge, for example, wrote an "open letter" to Norton (1985, 336–42) where she reflects on Norton's profound impact on her: first as a junior high-school student, then as a successful, adult writer. Vinge (1985, 338) notes that Norton's books are "written in a clean, straightforward prose that never gets in the way of its images, your adventures catch the elusive 'sense of wonder' that sets apart good science fiction from all other kinds of fiction and makes a fan into an addict." Vinge (1985, 342), like Norton's millions of fans, including me, concludes: "Because of you, I am."

Vinge's theme of Norton's transformative role as a mentor/author/ sponsor/person is reflected in Norton's work during the 1980s and 1990s with other authors in a series of anthologies—on the Witch World; on Ithkar, another unspecified, magical planet that exists in an unknown time; in the Star Ka'at series; and the catfantastic series (see references in Schlobin and Harrison 1995). Her coauthorship rapidly expanded her earlier patterns, too (Norton and Lackey 1991; Norton and Crispin 1984; Bradley, May, and Norton 1990; Bloch and Norton 1990).

CONCLUSION

The Year of the Unicorn is an exciting mythological adventure of a woman's journey to find a place in the Witch World as an adult, a wife, a witch, and a moral being. It is an exemplar of the "Norton formula," which alters patriarchal genre writing in fantasy and outer space.

Despite the recent growth in feminist scholarship in science fiction and tributes by other science-fiction writers, Norton remains "betwixt and between" popular culture and high culture; betwixt and between feminism and academic acceptance. This chapter documents the existence of the Norton formula, its debt to Baum's formula, and its scholarly background in the world literatures. Her ideas are more similar to "feminist pragmatism" than other popular types of feminist theories in hyper-modern America.

The Norton formula, moreover, has expanded through the work of other writers who use it and elaborate on it. I have no doubt that at some point, Norton's wide-ranging vision and cultural innovation will be lauded by a wide group of scholars. Until then, her millions of readers will continue to enjoy this great storyteller's tales of wonder and hope.

VI

Rapidly Changing American Rituals

11

The Ex-Wife at the Funeral

Agnes Riedmann

Because a significant number and proportion of contemporary American couples divorce, while a vast majority of ex-husbands remarry, women increasingly face the death of a remarried ex-spouse. Meanwhile, a former spouse may experience persistence of attachment after divorce (Weiss 1975): The "social construction of divorce" is a redefining process for former partners and takes time (Vaughan 1983, 1986). Furthermore, although voluntary ties with ex-partners may persist (Stacey 1990) and many of us experience ourselves as "relatives of divorce" (Johnson 1988), ex-kin are typically "defined out" of legal-rational definitions of the family (Schneider 1968, 23). Moreover, relationships between divorced ex-spouses are noninstitutionalized, thereby bereft of role prescription (Cherlin 1978, 1992; Price-Bonham and Balswick 1980; Stacey 1990). Consequently, the death and funeral of an ex-husband, particularly a remarried one, may prove problematic. As an ex-wife who participated in the funeral of her remarried ex-husband, I apply a case study methodological approach to a dramaturgical analysis of this ritual. Deegan's (1989a) core codes of the dramaturgical society are "inspected" (Blumer 1969, 43–47), and I propose a new concept—the *community production ritual*—for interpreting some contemporary American rituals.

DEATH AND FUNERALS IN AMERICAN SOCIETY

Research and other scholarly literature on death and dying in American society is characterized by the "acceptance-denial" controversy (Dumont and Foss 1972). From one perspective, Americans ignore death with a peculiar apathy (Gorer 1960, 1977; Kubler-Ross 1969; Glaser and Strauss 1965; Pattison 1977). In a syllogistic argument, Parsons (1967) suggests an opposite view. Because American society has institutionalized the values of science to a high degree and because a certain realism in facing the facts of the world is characteristic of the scientific attitude, it follows that death denial would be anomalous.

Dumont and Foss (1972, 1030) address this "cultural paradox" and conclude that "on a conscious, intellectual level the individual accepts his death, while on a generally unconscious, emotional plane" denying it. In a rational, progress- and action-oriented society such as ours, not all deaths—only unnecessary, preventable deaths or those defined as premature—are problematic. Premature deaths represent "unfinished business" (Blauner 1994, 39) and "may be seen as 'irrational' relative to the 'normal' natural aspects of death" (Parsons 1967, 138).

This "rationalization of death" impacts upon the dying (Glaser and Strauss 1965) and bereaved (Gorer 1977) and upon the contemporary funeral (Blauner 1994). For the bereaved, mourning becomes "grief work" to be accomplished privately and efficiently (Blackwood 1942; Kubler-Ross 1969; Bowman 1973). As an example, the subtitle of one grief advice book promises the reader "a sensible perspective for the modern person" (Marshall 1981).

Mandelbaum (1994, 361) characterizes American culture generally and the American funeral specifically as "deritualized." In premodern societies, the funeral ritual functioned as an "adaptive structure" (Blauner 1994, 450) to effect a renewed sense of belonging in which both family cohesion and kin relationships beyond the family were vividly demonstrated and reaffirmed (Mandelbaum 1994, 148–49). The contemporary funeral, in contrast, functions mainly as a complex status symbol (Bowman 1973) or impression-management vehicle for the funeral director (Pine 1975) and family. A result is that without the grief-healing balm of reintegrative ritual, death's "prospects and consequences become more serious for the bereaved individual" (Blauner 1994, 47). I argue that in contemporary American society, the funeral ritual is a "community production ritual" and, particularly when associated with an ex-husband's death, hardly reintegrative.

METHODOLOGY: CONDUCTING AN INADVERTENT BREACHING EXPERIMENT

This is an analysis based primarily on experiential observation. The author is the former wife of the deceased, to whom she had been married twenty-one years and from whom she had been divorced two years. The deceased had remarried.

One Thursday evening in August 1986, my twenty-one-year-old daughter, Anne (all family names have been changed in this chapter), called from her father's home to make a date with her brother, Joe, Jr., age nineteen, and me to see a movie. Fifty minutes later she called again. "Mom," she said, "get Joey right there with you."

"He's right here."

"Dad drowned in the pool," she said.

I participated in the structurally undefined role, *ex-spouse at the funeral*, from the time my daughter telephoned me from the hospital minutes after her father was pronounced dead on arrival through the days that followed. "What?" I screamed upon hearing the news. "Our dad is dead?" I felt the physical thump of shock. I began to tremble. Once off the phone, I paced rapidly in my kitchen for several minutes. That night I saw my ex-spouse as "our dad." I defined the situation as a "death in the (*our*, pre-divorced) family."

Not realizing in the initial hours that followed that others would define the situation otherwise, I spontaneously acted on that definition. For example, late that evening, feeling restless and in need of company, I visited my former mother-in-law's home. My ex-husband's younger brother, David, had arrived from his home out-of-town and would be staying there with his wife and three children. Even during and after the divorce, our relationships had remained congenial, if not friendly. I found my former in-laws receptive to me that evening. Neither they nor I had any idea of the dissension that was to come.

The next morning, Friday, I called my workplace to say I would not be there and to explain what had happened. Through the days that followed, I spoke with friends and relatives, some of the relatives lived long distances away, and encouraged them to come to support me.

Sometime that second day, as some people looked to me for direction in their expressions of sorrow and as I worried about my boss's reaction to any prolonged absence of mine from work, I realized that my definition of the situation was not taken for granted. Moreover, it became apparent that the stepfamily and my former in-laws were defining the situation differently than I was—as a death in only *their* family.

My daughter called twice that day. She had accompanied her stepmother and her Uncle David to the mortuary where they had made funeral arrangements. "You would like the casket we picked out," she told me the first time she called, and described it. She called later to tell me that "dad" would be buried in his blue pin-stripe suit. I responded that his tie should be diagonally striped and have the color maroon in it, reminding her that all his favorite ties were this way. "Well," she said, "I don't know. I feel so caught-in-the-middle. I shouldn't even have called you." Anne was to divide the next several days and nights between the homes of her paternal grandmother and her stepmother. I would not see or talk to her except at the public rituals that we both attended.

"He was forty-four," I made known often that day in response to the newspaper article and subsequent radio reports that had him at forty-five. "Why doesn't someone call the stations and tell them?" There was so much that others needed to know, it seemed, about the deceased and how he would probably want his funeral. I could help, I thought. But no one was asking. (Weeks later, a friend who had talked to me by telephone that day told me I had sounded "distraught.")

About noon my boss appeared. He had known me only since my divorce, and I sensed he was unsure how to respond. I was, too. I wondered how many days an "ex-" takes off work at a time like this. "The funeral is not until Monday," I said. "Take all the time you need," he offered, eyeing my son as he sobbed in an adjoining room. I realized that I was being excused partly as a bereaved child's mother.

An aunt and uncle of my former husband arrived. His godparents, they had been close to both of us through our courtship and marriage. They had come to my house, they explained, after having gone to Joe, Sr.'s mother's home. I realized at this point that three houses of mourning had developed: the deceased's mother's, his wife's, and mine. "We didn't know whether to stop," they said, "but we were going by and saw people on your front porch."

In the next few days, I attended the wake and funeral, went to the cemetery for the committal service, and afterward briefly visited the home of my former sister-in-law where family members gathered. In so doing, I inadvertently conducted a "breaching experiment."

Breaching experiments (Garfinkel 1963) are a methodological technique where the researcher breaks everyday rules, thereby discovering hidden nuances of the social order through resulting personal discomfort and/or external sanctions. I found myself and my definition of the situation "deviant" at the funeral services. For Goffman, embarrassment is the result of a failed performance; embarrassment indicates that one is somehow discredited or has breached norms and knows it. I was not only embarrassed, but I was also deeply offended and hurt during the days that followed my ex-husband's death. Since then I have analytically examined what occurred. I should add that friends and colleagues in sociology offered appreciated analytical insights, their purpose at that time to comfort me. These insights helped shape my later analytical thinking, although probably they did not motivate or change my behavior and attitudes during the experience.

THE COMMUNITY PRODUCTION RITUAL: THEORETICAL UNDERPINNINGS

Deegan (1978b, 1989a) synthesized anthropologist Victor Turner's and sociologist Erving Goffman's distinctively different work on ritual. Turner (1967), working primarily with nonmodern societies, views ritual as simultaneously personally liberating and socially integrative. For Goffman, studying contemporary everyday life, rituals are minute and inauthentic procedures by which individuals—ever-worried about impression management—present themselves as creditable.

Goffman minutely details the everyday process of continual defense of the self *against* the other, while Turner explicates the process of finding a sense of self and community *with* the other (Deegan 1978b). For Turner (1967), ritual participants leave everyday life to enter a liminal world in which ordinary social structure is temporarily suspended: They are "betwixt and between." In this *anti-structure*, "concrete, historical, and idiosyncratic individuals" experience renewal, creativity, refreshment. Bonds of *communitas* result—anti-structural in the sense that they are undifferentiated, equalitarian, direct, nonrational (though not irrational), I-Thou relationships (Turner 1967, 49, 53). For Goffman (1959, 1963, 1974), in contrast, action is staged by performers. "Any arbitrary slice or cut from the stream of ongoing activity" is a performance "strip" governed by principles of organization called a "frame." A frame can be altered—keyed and rekeyed—to enhance a performance (Goffman 1974, 10–11, 45–83). The self is essentially a "performed character," a "product of a scene that comes off; . . . a person is a dramatic effect, arising diffusely from a scene that is presented and the characteristic issue, the crucial concern, is whether it will be credited or discredited" (Goffman 1959, 252–53). Put another way, the individual is alienated.

Deegan (1989a) integrated concepts from Turner and Goffman to create the concept "anti-structure frame." The anti-structure frame marks a strip of ritual experience in modern life, but it is not alienating. Unfortunately, albeit not surprisingly, Deegan finds few anti-structure frames in contemporary American life. In a former paper (Riedmann 1988) and in an analysis similar to Deegan's, I proposed the original, empirically grounded concept, "keyed anti-structure." As I use it, keyed anti-structure denotes contemporary ceremonial rituals as removed from the everyday and as emotionally charged. Ritual participants are "concrete, historical, and idiosyncratic individuals" in need of renewal. At the same time, keyed anti-structure recognizes participants' dramaturgically contrived and inauthentic performances.

The concept, keyed anti-structure, led me to a second concept, "community production rituals," explicated for the first time in this chapter. In her critical analysis of American "fun times," Deegan divided rituals into two types: participatory and media-constructed (see chapter 1). Here I propose a third ritual type, the "community production ritual." Having elements from each of Deegan's ritual types, the community production ritual involves the performance of the common person, not a professional actor, in a socially constructed event or fiction presented to the community.

Often the impression to be conveyed is the financial success or high status of ritual participants. Community production rituals are typically executed during rites of passage. In any rite of passage, something is personally lost even as something else may be gained. Hence, in Turner's communitas, rituals surrounding rites of passage function to restore or heal participants. In contemporary American society, however, rituals that accompany rites of passage incorporate alienating elements of contrived participatory theater.

THE AMERICAN FUNERAL RITUAL AS ANTI-STRUCTURAL

The American funeral ritual is anti-structural inasmuch as some "everyday" rules are suspended. Employees, depending upon the closeness of their relationship to the deceased, are excused from work after the death occurs until sometime after the funeral.[1] A good portion of this time can be characterized by conviviality, if not joviality. Good food—and often drink—is shared; old friendships are renewed. Typically, this mood climaxes at the wake (Bowman 1973). My colleagues and friends, along with friends who had known my former husband and me as a couple, began to congregate at my home. Someone did dishes and cleaned the kitchen. Someone else began to answer the phone and take messages. Flowers arrived.

This "time out" persists in our society as recognition of individuals as more than actors in a specific role in everyday life. They are a person embarking on a period of grief. Death, after all, breaks relationships in a way that necessitates a reconstruction of lives and a change in the everyday understandings that guide interaction. "Some persons describe the gripping experience as one of being suddenly and utterly alone, while looking straight into the great unknown" (Bendiksen 1994, 59). In grief, people experience themselves as "betwixt and between" the world they had taken for granted and some new reality not yet defined. In this liminal stage, the grief-stricken desire "the sense of equality among friends. The craving is for acceptance of themselves without reservation as well as for the uninhibited giving of affection" (Bowman 1973, 143). Put another way, the grief-stricken require communitas.

The anti-structural "time out" given for death in our society can generate communitas. But the American funeral is a community production ritual that functions as a vehicle for reification of our legal-rationally structured system. This may be particularly apparent to the divorced person. For example, those who can openly or legitimately mourn, that is, the "survivors," are legal-rationally defined. While the anti-structural element of the contemporary funeral ritual allows persons free time absent from some "everyday" rules such as productivity in work, building communitas is not culturally defined as its purpose. Operating in this vacuum, individuals may have still greater occasion and opportunity to create performance teams than they do in everyday interaction. They can contrive their "personal fronts," for example, with greater deliberation.

THE AMERICAN FUNERAL RITUAL AS KEYED

Ours is a bureaucratically structured society (Deegan 1989a), and burial in America is legal-rationally keyed. Especially for males, status and achievement is publicly applauded. On some level, this was apparent to me from the time I first read the newspaper report of the drowning through my urging that the deceased wear the proper tie and my subsequent appreciation for the expensive walnut coffin. Furthermore, I calculated my dress and style or "personal front." I scheduled a haircut. ("Every ex-wife should look great at her ex-husband's funeral!" my hairdresser of several years cheered.) That afternoon I planned how I would dress. I chose stylish, upper-middle-class clothes—things I rarely found occasion to wear anymore. I would look like a (former) lawyer's wife—rather than like a graduate student in sociology. One element of the "personal front," particularly important in the ceremonial key (Goffman 1974, 58), is appearance, functioning "to tell us of the performer's social statuses" (Goffman 1959, 24).

Not only professional success but family solidarity is applauded. In Talcott Parson's and Victor Lidz's (1967, 142) words:

Deaths, like other major points of transition in the personal life cycle, remain occasions upon which the central significance of the nuclear family in the personal attachments of the individuals is conspicuously demonstrated, along with the solidarity of the more extended kin groups.

In our society, family bonds, while admittedly affectional and nomos-generating (Berger and Kellner 1970), are legal-rationally defined. The obituary notice, which omitted any reference to an ex-wife, made this clear. Listing the appropriate team members as it did, the notice became a public playbill or "formula" (Cawelti 1969, 386) to facilitate legitimate rekeying. But in this particular community production, we were mourning a "successful" man, and for that reason among others, I wanted to be on the team.

Teams perform in the context of frames. In Goffman's dichotomy, strips of experience can be purely physical "natural frames" or "social frames" and directed. In addition, social experience is "laminated"—transformed or systematically altered through the process of keying and rekeying (Goffman 1974, 43–44). A ceremony is one of several kinds of keys. Death in its purely physical sense is a natural frame; disposal of the body introduces a social frame, that is laminated or keyed by the burial ceremony.

Performance Teams

Performance teams emerged. Performance teams involve participants' cooperative "collusion" to sustain or impose one of many possibly competing definitions of the situation upon an audience (Goffman 1959, 80). Teams can perform not only before an audience, but also competitively with one another. In this latter situation, one team becomes an audience for the other, and vice-versa, and the teams battle to win the other over and/or for the allegiance of still a third group.

Sometime Saturday, two days after the drowning, I drove my mother to my former mother-in-law's. I thought they could share their common grief. But the latter appeared anxious at our arrival, and we did not stay long. While we were there, one of my former in-laws mentioned going to the mortuary for the family viewing. Anxious to see the body, I asked whether I could go. "It's not a time for strangers to go," my former mother-in-law answered. It was agreed that my son and I would visit the mortuary for a private viewing that evening. I went with my son partly because—it was explained—only members of the deceased's family or those accompanying them could visit the funeral home at a publicly unscheduled hour. Since I was not a member of the family team, my son would gain entry for me.

The casket, a rich walnut, was closed. A large, recent portrait of the deceased and his children hung above it. On the left was a collection of photographs of the deceased and of him with his children. These pictures had been taken in earlier days. He had compiled this collection after our divorce, and it had been hanging in his law office. I noted that while I was expectedly not in any of these pictures, I had taken several of them.

Alone with the body, my son and I eventually began to inspect the flowers surrounding the casket. I noted that one bouquet, displayed prominently, had been sent by the republican congressional representative.

"That embarrasses me," I said to my son, thinking of my politically liberal friends who might be attending the wake. We removed the signature tag.

Meanwhile, the obituary notice exacerbated the development of separate mourning teams. As early as Friday, the day after the drowning, competing teams had begun to develop. Groups had established separate houses of mourning or backstages where, among other things, teammates would declare allegiance and create their respective "fronts." For example, upon reading the obituary, my son, fully on my team, consoled me. Ultimately, distinct teams fully emerged: the *family* team and the *ex-family* team. Each competed to impose its definition of the situation as the "real-family" team.

At the wake, many friends, both my own and those who had known us as a couple, met with me. Some seemed surprised to see me there. Of the surprised, some appeared disconcerted and others appeared relieved or pleased. Many, perhaps the majority, did not know the deceased's second wife and drifted to me to share memories. Not having been assigned a place to sit and uncomfortable with my ambiguous position, I wandered into the mortuary lobby before the service. As people entered, many stopped there to visit with me. "Anne was born the night of our labor law exam," an old school buddy reminisced. "Joe thought that was great! You in labor and him in labor law." Eyeing my daughter, another attorney remarked that she was "good-looking," then added that "She looks like both of you." "That's why she's good-looking," I returned.

During the service, we were told that the deceased had two children and had been a formidable trial attorney and a "family man." No mention was made of his having been divorced and remarried. The family team, having contracted the funeral and supported by social structure, strategically controlled the ceremonial settings. (I, meanwhile, took control of the mortuary lobby.) Control of setting is an advantage because it affords control over what information the audience receives (Goffman 1959, 91–93). The mortuary setting includes flowers, music, furniture, decor, physical layout, and other background items or scenery (Goffman 1959, 22), all accenting the primary ceremonial symbol, the prepared body lying in a casket. The family team controlled attributes of the primary symbol, such as clothing and coffin style, along with supporting symbols, such as the portrait and photographs. These latter helped define the situation of the deceased as a "family man" without any meaningful relationship to his ex-wife.

Several friends telephoned me after the funeral to complain and share their frustration. "How does it feel to be the invisible woman?" a former neighbor of ours asked. "They made it sound like he went through law school single," I protested. Weeks later I confided to a sociologist friend, whom I had known nearly thirteen years and who had attended the wake, that I felt guilty about having somewhat purposefully "worked the crowd" that night. He replied that "one performance deserved the other."

The Team Director

Initially, the stepfamily and my former in-laws may have hoped that I would attend the funeral services—if at all—only as an interested member of the larger community. When it became evident that I planned to join the mourning team publicly, the deceased's brother David emerged as director.

Because in a team performance any member can "give the show away," a director may emerge whose responsibility it is to ensure against this. The director's duties involve "bringing back into line any member of the team whose performance becomes unsuitable, typically by soothing and sanctioning" (Goffman 1959, 98). As uncle to my children and brother of the deceased, David moved between the separate houses of mourning to carry messages and ensure that no problems were arising. Even through my performance at the wake, characterized by a "haughty" and threatening "manner" (Goffman 1959, 24), the family team defined all of us, albeit tentatively, as fellow mourners with the common dramaturgical goal of a smooth performance.

Before we left the mortuary that night, David appeared at my side and began to rub my back. Shortly thereafter he remarked that "we don't want any trouble tomorrow." The director's soothing and sanctioning failed in its purpose. Indeed, thereafter I took more active direction of what I now definitely perceived as "my team," while allowing my ex-husband's brother Carl the role of co-captain or second-in-command.

After I returned home from the wake, Carl called to say that he and his wife would drive me to the funeral service in the morning. It meant that he would not ride with his mother and siblings. I accepted this offer gratefully, aware that he risked subsequent alienation from his blood relatives. Carl, younger than Joe, and his wife and Joe and I had for many years been a "foursome," particularly on weekend afternoons.

My daughter, I had learned, would neither walk with me in the funeral procession into the church nor sit near me during the ceremony. As a member of the family, she would lead the procession immediately behind the casket. I, not a member of the family, would be expected to walk farther back. By now I felt that I had lost not only my ex-spouse but also my daughter.

The funeral ceremony proceeded much as had the wake. I dressed similarly and attended as the deceased's first or ex-wife. Not assigned a place to sit with the family, I sat with friends on the left of the church toward the front. My son, along with his father's law partners, would be a pallbearer. I sat behind and close to him. Throughout the service, I sobbed and shook, feeling physically cold even as I perspired. After the ceremony, Carl ushered me into his car and aggressively maneuvered his way into the funeral procession to the cemetery just behind the one family limousine. As we drove, he played a tape of Cher. "Remember that?" he asked. "Remember when we all went to see Cher?"

Discredited

At the cemetery, someone requested, surprisingly to me, that only the family remain for the committal service. The legal family controlled the space under the cemetery tent, which had been pitched to enclose the committal service. Unwelcome guests (members of competing teams) could be asked to leave as I was. In an emotional outbreak, I ran from the area, yelling "Fuck it!" My relatives and Carl's wife followed. After I composed myself, we walked slowly back to the grave. By this time the family had been ushered quickly into the mortuary limousine. The grave diggers were leaning close, wanting to get to work but wondering whether to begin with people still watching. I asked them to wait a few minutes, approached the casket, said my final "goodbye," then told them to go ahead. Afterward, Carl and his wife drove me to the house where the family was to gather for the afternoon. I sensed upon entering that I was not welcome. I explained that I had come to pick up my son, and subsequently the two of us left. We spent the afternoon with my relatives.

THE CORE CODES OF THE AMERICAN DRAMATURGICAL SOCIETY

As Young and Massey (1978, 78) define it, the dramaturgical society is one in which "the technologies of social science, mass communication, theater, and the arts are used to manage attitudes, behaviors, and feelings of the population in modern mass society" (cited in Deegan 1989a, 19). Deegan's four core codes of the American dramaturgical society (see chapter 1) are manifest in my data. This analysis of the ex-wife—mourning but "defined out"—at the funeral has explicated processes by which rationalized social structure is alienating. In a bureaucratized society, individuals become increasingly dependent on a "private world" in hopes of finding a restorative "home" for their emotional selves (Berger, Berger, and Kellner 1973). What experience could seem more private than a death in the family? But in a dramaturgical society, the Weberian (1958/1920) iron cage imprisons the private as well as the public world. In my case study, a result was the "hidden sorrow" of "disenfranchised grief" (Doka 1989), a peculiarly modern condition in which only those defined as legitimate mourners grieve without negative sanction. This disenfranchisement of grief is exacerbated by capitalism. In a capitalistic society, the funeral ritual is a purchased event while the owner of the means of the ceremonial production wields control over it. In my data, the family team, having financed the funeral, contrived the ritual settings. The funeral director and staff support this team.

Furthermore, the control and use of time has become rationalized in contemporary society. With time commodified, we "spend" it; an activity becomes "worth so much time." Meanwhile, time-constrained individuals are expected to prioritize work or employment activities. Even for enfranchised "survivors," legitimately entering the anti-structure of mourning, grief is "worth so much" time out. When my boss offered me "all the time you need," I felt grateful. All the time I needed exceeded his assumptions, however. Having returned to work the second day after the funeral, I found myself crying at the water cooler and went home to sit for a week on my front porch. I spent the time refusing phone calls, staring across the street, and going for short walks after which I found myself thoroughly exhausted. When I returned to work the second time, I was informed of my boss's concern as he needed "someone who can be reliable in this position."

Meanwhile, a fourth core code, the sex code, confirms gender stereotypes and the structured arrangement between the sexes. Even in a society characterized by changing gender roles, the status of wife, particularly the wife of a "successful" husband, remains a cherished one. My impulsive attempt to perform that role at the funeral confirmed as much, publicly and personally. I was, after all, a full-time employee and a doctoral student seriously embarked on attaining my own independent status as an academic. But at this ritual, my status as wife and helpmate to the deceased (I had put him through law school, you may recall) became paramount.

THE COMMUNITY PRODUCTION RITUAL AND ITS FAILURE TO RESTORE

Interacting, the four codes—sexism, time commodification, capitalism, and bureaucracy—form "a united system of rules for alienating the self from the other" (Deegan 1989a, 20). Ritual actors, their experiences and emotions depreciated by both external and internal censoring, feel oppressed and repressed (Deegan 1989a, 20–21). Moreover, when in a dramaturgical society community rituals become community production rituals, participants not only feel alienated, but they behave in inauthentic, even cruel, ways: "As people, we cannot imagine how we could transcend everyday life without being unfair and controlling" (Deegan 1989a, 157).

Even as I felt engulfed by grief, I contrived my performance and behaved inauthentically. But death is profoundly more than the exit of an important actor and his or her subsequent symbolization in a ceremonially keyed frame. Grief hurts. People shake and sweat. In addition, life events occurred, the emotional ramifications of which exacerbated my sorrow. I had virtually lost a daughter, at least for the time being; my brother-in-law Carl risked severed ties from his family of orientation. My two children, who could have been peculiarly mutually supportive during this time, barely saw each other. My brother-in-law David and I, who had always been good friends, were alienated. David had always been my son's favorite uncle; to this day, my son remains ambivalent about him. All this compounded my aloneness. Deegan has reminded us that Herbert Marcuse (1956, cited in Deegan 1989a, 153–55) characterized experiences such as mine as "surplus repression"—the social creation and maintenance of unnecessary suffering. Due to the core codes of a dramaturgical society, incorporated as they are into American ritual life, "ritual structure is corrupted in a 'surplus' way that mirrors our mundane existence" (Deegan 1989a, 153).

CONCLUSION

In our core-coded dramaturgical society, the funeral of an ex-spouse is potentially problematic. This situation provided a setting for a case study that can be characterized as an inadvertent "breaching experiment." My analysis has produced the original concept of the community production ritual, with the funeral as one example.

Mandelbaum (1994) described the American funeral as "deritualized." This characterization is unerring inasmuch as we use Victor Turner's definitional requirement that ritual be necessarily reintegrative and restorative. However, Mandelbaum's analysis of the contemporary American funeral as deritualized is not accurate from Goffman's perspective, which views rituals as everyday life performances. I have shown that the contemporary American funeral functions as a complex status symbol or impression-management vehicle for those who finance it. Put another way, the American funeral today is a community production ritual, characterized by keyed anti-structure. Especially for disenfranchised grievers, attending a funeral is unlikely to be restorative or to offer communitas. As a community production ritual, the contemporary American funeral may indeed cause "surplus repression" and the concomitant compounding of grief.

NOTE

1. [The time allowed off from work varies by occupation and by social class. Exploring the interactions of time, class, bureaucracy, gender, and race concerning this issue is beyond the scope of this chapter. I was horrified, however,

when a clerical worker in the department of sociology at the University of Chicago, when I was a student there in the 1970s, was expected back at work the day after her parent's funeral. When she asked for more time off, her request was refused. I saw her that day and she was barely able to function and was petrified that she would lose her job. A friend and untenured colleague was not allowed to cancel his classes after his mother's funeral at still another university—ed. note.]

12

Quinceañera: The Mexican–American Initiation Ritual of Young Women

Bert Watters

My spouse and I became curious about the quinceañera ritual after seeing a "bloopers" program on Spanish-language TV called *Camera Infragante*.[1] These home videos depicted young Mexican girls in elaborate white dresses and young boys in formal dress accidentally falling on top of each other while dancing, and white dresses catching fire or flying up to reveal the young women's unmentionables. Besides the real-life "humor" of these scenes, we wondered what exactly occurred before and during this celebration (and its inadvertent mayhem). I wanted to understand the purpose of the quinceañera, the details of the ritual process, its "fit" in today's cultural context, and why I and many other Mexican-American women[2] do not participate in it. These questions are asked by many young, first-generation and later generations of Mexican-American women who did not pass through the quinceañera ritual.

Many dimensions of this ritual, such as its history, religion, and issues of gender and modernity, are rarely overtly addressed by the Mexican-American community. Here, I analyze the ritual with the aid of three social theorists: Victor Turner, Mary Jo Deegan, and Norma Williams. My analysis of the quinceañera ritual focuses on how it creates different levels or degrees of Turner's *communitas* for those involved; how it expresses and perpetuates Deegan's sex and age core codes; and, finally, how Williams's concepts show that the quinceañera ritual is perceived by young Mexican-American women who are separating themselves from this ritual and creating a new social identity.

The quinceañera is a celebration, a rite of passage (Van Gennepp 1960), that marks a young Mexican-American girl's entry into adulthood at the age of fifteen. Extended families, the Roman Catholic church, and the community join together to create the ceremony and the reception that follows it. Once the young girl goes through this ritual, she is viewed as a woman and is expected to accept all the responsibilities and behaviors that accompany her new status.

METHODOLOGY

Research on this ritual is sparse. There are allusions to the quinceañera ritual in various books on Mexican folklore and in publications that emphasize the Mexican-American experience and issues. Mary Lankford (1994), however, has published a small volume on the quinceañera, specifically for the young girls preparing for this ritual. She presents pictures and a text that follows the ritual through the various stages that a fictional participant—Martha Jimenez—experiences. Lankford does not emphasize the ritual's origins, its symbolic meaning, its impact on the female participant, or its future survival. Nonetheless, she does provide a foundation for and a valuable explanation of the principle stages of the quinceañera.

Due to the scarcity of available materials on this ritual, I also relied on qualitative techniques to gather information on this rite of passage. I obtained video footage and photographs of a quinceañera that took place in a small midwestern city in 1992. I also interviewed two Mexican-American women with first-hand experience of the quinceañera to obtain more information about the process and to discuss their opinions of the ritual and its future in the United States and in Mexico.

THE QUINCEAÑERA RITUAL

The quinceañera involves many aspects of everyday life such as the church and family. Usually, the ceremony is performed in a Roman Catholic church with a reception immediately following that continues the ritual. Months of preparation involve the dresses the girls will wear, the church ceremony, the reception afterward, and the participation of the extended family and friends. Due to the expense of the quinceañera (it can cost thousands of dollars), relatives and friends usually assist in coordinating the event and the expenses.

The young girl, typically, has an escort and a group of attendants for the day. The latter group is called a *corte de honor* and is composed of fourteen pairs of *chambelanes* and *damas* (chamberlains and ladies) who escort the young girl throughout the ceremony. These couples must themselves be at or close to fifteen years of age and unmarried. The young girl also has an escort for the day, making a total of fifteen pairs, where each pair symbolizes a year of the girl's life.

The *corte de honor*, her family, and her friends gather at the church where they await the young girl. She arrives in a decorated car, dressed in an elaborate white dress similar to a wedding gown (this type of dress is also seen in the First Communion rite in the Catholic Church, when young girls officially enter the church). In the church ceremony, the fourteen pairs of *damas* and *chambelanes* walk down the church aisle, followed by the young girl and her parents. After this entrance, a church service is held in honor of the fifteen-year-old girl. The parents present the girl with gifts, including rosary beads, a prayer book, and jewelry. During the service, the girl reaffirms and promises to continue her faith by restating her baptismal and confirmation vows, taking the Eucharist and offering roses on the altar of the Virgin Mary. After the service, everyone goes to a hall where a reception is held (again, similar to a wedding reception) and the quinceañera ritual continues.

At the hall, the *corte de honor* enters the dance area through an archway and forms a corridor for the young woman and her escort. The couples are followed by the girl's parents who carry a pair of white high-heeled shoes. The young woman then sits on an elevated chair, where the father places the white shoes on his daughter's feet. She rises from the chair and proceeds to dance with her father, who symbolically introduces the young woman to all those present at the reception, continuing her rite of passage from childhood to adulthood. The young woman's *chambelane de honor* steps in and continues the dance. What follows is a criss-cross dance pattern where the young woman and her *chambelane de honor* take turns dancing with each member of the *corte* (Lankford 1994).

THEORETICAL ANALYSIS

The quinceañera ritual comprises various levels of interactive meaning. On the surface, it celebrates the coming of age of Mexican-American girls, a rite of passage into adulthood witnessed by the family and the community. Turner extensively studied rite-of-passage rituals, and he drew on the earlier studies of Arnold Van Gennep. Van Gennep coined the phrase "rite de passage" for rites of transition and defined them as "rites which accompany every change of place, state, social position and age" (Turner 1977, 36). Turner (1977, 36–37) describes Van Gennep's ritual phases as follows:

Rites of transition are marked by three phases: separation; margin (or limen); and re-aggregation. The first and last detach ritual subjects from their old places in society and return them, inwardly transformed and outwardly changed, to new places. Limen is a threshold, a pilgrims road, or passing from dynamics to statics.

The liminal phase is the transitional stage of the ritual, or what Turner calls a "betwixt and between" status.

The betwixt-and-between phase of the ritual is pivotal because it unites the self and the other. "Communitas" is established, thereby, when the interaction of the self (the initiant) with the other (society) becomes one in community. Communitas is the bond between the sacred and the mundane that connects the self and the other in everyday life. In *The Ritual Process*, Turner (1969, 47) analyzes initiation rituals that create anti-structure and communitas. During rituals, groups withdraw from everyday life to create communitas. Individuals with similar backgrounds, cultures, religions, or ethnicity join others who share the same cultural features. In my analysis, the quinceañera is a catalyst for communitas to emerge among and between extended families and within the Mexican-American community.

In *American Ritual Dramas*, Deegan (1989a) builds on the work of Turner, but in a hyper-modern society. She identifies core codes that unite and interact with one another to alienate the self from the other, thus creating an oppressive and repressive state for the self and others involved (see further discussion of core codes in chapter 1). I concentrate here on the sex and age codes in the quinceañera ceremony.

In studying ritual interactions, Deegan shows that the sex core code, like class, is one of the most prevalent codes and is deeply ingrained in our daily lives. This sex code can be blatant (see Deegan's analysis of "The Meet/Meat Market Ritual") or barely noticeable within a particular ritual. The sex code can be pervasive in the culture and can be accepted and practiced by all participants until other outside factors have an impact on the individuals and the culture. In the case of the Mexican-American culture, the process of disassociation and/or acculturation by succeeding generations reflects such an outside influence.

An age core code is a pattern used in a culture's rituals that oppresses or represses individuals based on their position in the life-course. This code tends to be particularly problematic for persons at the extreme ends of the age spectrum. However, the exact chronological ages that fix the limits of the spectrum are becoming more and more undefined due to the modern extended life expectancy. The age code within a culture is an evaluation of a person's (re)productive worth, physical appearance, ability, or maturity. In the case of the quinceañera ritual, the age code identifies fifteen years as the appropriate age to begin a new stage of life—adulthood—and also places a high value on this age for women.

Life-cycle rituals like the quinceañera announce to the participant and others that a major shift in her roles is in order: The young girl becomes a woman with all the privileges and responsibilities that encompass the role of an adult woman. But role expectations of young Mexican-American women have changed in response to educational, personal, and career success. This is a major shift from just a few decades ago.

Williams, a symbolic interactionist, writes about the social and cultural forces that have had an impact, directly and indirectly, in recent decades on the restructuring of the Mexican-American family. Increased urbanization and acculturation, in particular, have deeply affected Mexican-American women's social roles. These roles have been changed, too, by the expectation of increasing education, work in the paid labor force, and the need to establish an individual social identity. Thus, women in the marketplace who break from the homemaker's traditional role and who increase their education directly impact their financial future. Education and financial liberation combine to create a variety of cultural value shifts that further complicate their futures. A new value system has been fostered, thereby, in which young Mexican-American women support a "new individualism." The focus of young women has increasingly changed from marriage, motherhood, and dependence on their spouses to one where their own lives are a primary concern (Turner 1976). Simultaneously, there is less emphasis on or commitment to religion and its traditional role for women.

The civil rights movement has also been a catalyst for young Mexican-American women struggling for greater social equality, which affects the family's structure and dynamics as well as the traditional roles and rituals of Mexican-American women. Mexican-American women are responding to changes in their social and cultural environment and thereby altering expectations for their younger counterparts. Young Mexican-American women no longer wish to be "twice a minority," one in the Mexican culture and another in the American culture (Williams 1990, 5–7).

Because of the changes in expectations and roles in this hyper-modern society, there is a cultural disassociation or selective acculturation occurring among urbanized Mexican-American women. Young, urbanized Mexican-American women have attached a different meaning to the quinceañera ritual: from one of initiation into adulthood and all the responsibilities associated with it, to one of oppression of the woman, limiting her choices and potential growth in today's society (Williams 1990, 41). Williams uses empirical findings to illustrate contemporary Mexican-American family life and how members of the working and professional class are defining and redefining traditions, rituals, and changes in the Mexican-American culture. I carry this a step further to see if or how the quinceañera "fits" in today's context for young Mexican-American girls.

DISCUSSION

Communitas and the Quinceañera

There are many months of preparation and expenses incurred for the quinceañera. Extended family and community members are invited to participate and/or observe the ritual passage of the young girl into adulthood; with this ceremony, communitas is created. Initially, there is a liminal phase, which is an "extraordinary world created and entered through the ritual process" (Deegan 1989a, 9); namely, the quinceañera. This liminal phase "reveals both the individual and the group in a personally and emotionally complex way" (Deegan 1989a, 9). Communitas emerges from the experience of the young girl and her family/friends who are one in community for and during the quinceañera ritual procession. It is a unifying experience for all the Mexican-Americans involved. Turner (1977, 47) states:

In our society, it seems that the small groups which nourish communitas, do so by withdrawing voluntarily from the mainstream not only of economic but also of domestic familial life. . . . People who are similar in one important characteristic—sex, age, ethnicity, [or] religion—withdraw symbolically from the total system to seek the glow of communitas among those with whom they share some cultural or biological feature they take to be their most signal mark of identity.

This ritual process occurs when the quinceañera brings together the Mexican-American community (which itself is alienated from the dominant American culture) to celebrate the new adult status of the young celebrant.

The initiant goes through what Turner (1977, 44) calls a betwixt-and-between phase during the ritual. This midtransition point, or liminal zone, calls attention to certain universal, symbolic structures within the quinceañera. The liminal zone tends to be concerned with calendrical (the fifteen-year point in this female's life), biological (the physiological maturity of the female to bear children), and social-structural (introduction or initiation into the community) cycles of the young girl's life in the flow of sociocultural processes.

The couples, or *corte de honor*, also go through the liminal process in that they symbolically represent each year of the girl's life as they progress through the ritual. Communitas develops while they creat this symbolic representation of the fifteen years, which permits a "communion of equal individuals" (Bruce Lincoln 1981, 103) to unite. These couples also resemble the couples in a wedding procession, that is the bride's maids and their partners. These fifteen-year-old couples are usually the sons and daughters of the other participating extended families.

Lastly, communitas is created by uniting the extended family and community to participate in and observe the event. The extended family and community join together in this liminal zone to witness and celebrate the young girl who is making her personal journey through the quinceañera. Communitas is established as all these participants go through the initiation rite (the church service and reception) that again draws attention to the universal and symbolic structures discussed here. Extended family members may contribute financially to the pre-ceremony and ceremony preparation, depending upon the young girls' economic status. They may be responsible for certain activities and events, as well as for food, hall rental, or entertainment. All guests contribute, whether in the form of materials, money, or attendance at the event, especially those representatives of other extended families—potential marriage partners for the newly initiated woman.

The Core Codes

The Sex Core Code and the Quinceañera

The quinceañera originated in the everyday life of the Aztecs of ancient Mexico. The women's role in the culture was limited, as was the destiny of the young girls who usually at the age of twelve or thirteen (the years when puberty begins) attended one of two schools, depending upon their future role in the Aztec society. There was the *Calmacac* school, which prepared the young girls for religious service, and the *Telpucucali*, which prepared the girls for marriage. The initiation rites stressed chastity, truthfulness, and obedience.

After the Spanish conquered the Aztec empire, the indigenous rituals and traditions for women merged with Catholic indoctrination to create a unique ritual for young girls in their passage to womanhood. Formerly, the young girls were encouraged to decide between marriage or a religious life as a nun. In this modern day, however, the decision has evolved to choosing between remaining single or becoming married.

The formalized ceremony of ritual and celebration for passage from childhood to adulthood—the quinceañera—applies to females only: There is no comparable ritual for males in the Mexican culture. The sex core code applies to the fundamental function of everyday life of a young girl's rite of passage that traditionally limits her options in life to marriage and motherhood.

Another aspect of this ritual's sex code is its association with the age at which girls enter puberty and develop bodies that are, or soon will be, capable of bearing children. This initiation into adulthood stresses the difference between a child's asexual identification and an adult's sexual identification. This ritual demonstrates that young girls are being pre-pared for heterosexual relations. Then, as now, the priority of having children is stressed from early childhood to the quinceañera and beyond. Raised by the extended family (which participates in the ceremony), the soon-to-be women must go outside the group for sexual partners to start families. The rite brings together members from other extended families that may offer a potential partner for the young girl (Vizedom 1976, 35–36). This quinceañera ritual can be viewed as a rehearsal for the wed-ding ceremony that will take place, sooner rather than later, with a part-ner from one of the other participating families.

Many nonmodern female rites-of-passage ceremonies involve special clothing and/or body adornment, as in the white dress and shoes worn by the young girl and the jewelry presented to her by her parents. The white dress alludes to the purity/virginity of the young girl, as does a white dress worn by a bride. This contrasts with men's adolescent rituals: Boys go from being a child to entering a higher public status, but women re-main in the female world. The body is not transformed through scarring or other male, public signs of adulthood status, but the girl's internal changes are symbolized through her clothing and accessories. Rather than changing only the girl's public status, the rite of passage changes her fundamental being: It addresses her essential nature, not just her social position in the Mexican culture. This is a sex core code in action within the Mexican culture.

The quinceañera ritual marks the child's growth into adulthood sym-bolically, as in the white dress and shoes of a future bride, and literally, through physical maturity to marry and bear children (Bruce Lincoln 1981). The ritual announces the next step into the inevitable fate of a young woman as wife and mother, whether she wills it or not.

In many ways, the quinceañera is the Mexican version of a "coming out" ceremony for a young Anglo debutant: a girl is displayed to the com-munity in general and to eligible males in particular. The white dress and high-heeled shoes foreshadow a bride-to-be: a reaffirmation of faith and an association with a virgin (the Virgin Mother of God in the church service). The ceremonial dance with each *chambelane*, moreover, allows the young men to meet the newly initiated women up close. These are only a few examples of the sex code that shapes the young woman enter-ing a predetermined role of womanhood in Mexican society.

The Age Core Code and the Quinceañera

Literally interpreted, quinceañera in Spanish means "quince" (fif-teen) and "años" (years or birthday). Deegan's core codes are "basic com-ponent[s] of everyday structures that oppress and repress" (Deegan 1989, 20), and the age code functions here as a hallmark to begin external impositions of marriage and assumption of other womanly responsibilities. Is this an appropriate age to enter adulthood ritually and literally? To begin thinking of marriage and facing other adult issues?

The answers, I believe, are "no." This age does not fit the hypermodern (Giddens 1990) context of appropriate behavior and issues for fifteen-year-old girls. Reflecting upon the Aztec origins of this ritual, it was reasonable to expect marriage at a young age in a society with short life expectancies. Puberty would begin during that time period at fourteen or fifteen, which was the chronological half-life of the typical Aztec women who chose to enter the *Telpucucali*. With the modern life expectancy of 85+ years for women in today's global community, the juxtaposition of 15 years as a benchmark in an age of maturity and halfway point in one's life cycle seems perverse. With the technology, economics, and life-style of modern society, eighteen or twenty years of age might be a more appropriate age to make choices as an adult that have lifelong impact. Transposing the quinceañera ritual onto today's social context, it imposes coded social responsibilities at a very early age and severely narrows the girls' potential opportunities.

The age at which one is legally allowed to engage in sexual activity, in the United States at least, is older than just fifteen years. The law has stated a certain age (eighteen years) as acceptable to engage in marital sexual activity, which has been dictated by accepted social norms. At the quinceañera, however, the young girl is initiated into womanhood with all the traditional responsibilities associated with it: marriage, children, and respect for and subserviance to the male. The age code associated with the quinceañera definitely conflicts with today's social norms and practices concerning sexual activity for young girls, especially if the sexual act is intended for procreation. One should not ignore the fact that young Mexican-American women engage in sexual activity at a young age; however, premarital sexual activity is considered taboo not only in Mexican society, but especially in strict Roman Catholic teaching (which plays an integral part of Mexican society, as well as in the quinceañera ritual).

The issues of age and educational career conflict in today's social context as well. Education is emphasized more and more as a key to the advancement of young Mexican-American women in the United States and in developing Latin countries. Yet the quinceañera ritual announces that the young woman is ready for her adult and family roles in that society. As recently as sixty years ago, education for the young Mexican-American woman was not stressed. Society in general would have considered the equivalency of a fifth-grade education as all that was needed to function in Mexican society. In today's context, the young Mexican-American female is expected to complete high school to function at a minimal level. In more urban or affluent areas, they are expected to continue far beyond high school to city college and/or university and to enter the work force at a competitive level and attain occupational success. With the age code in effect in this ritual, education is neither a consideration nor is it relevant to this young woman's social role.

Financial independence complements education as a criterion to function minimally in today's society, and it aids in creating a social identity. At the age of fifteen, the young Mexican-American girl may be considered a woman: However, she is still dependent upon her parents or a soon-to-be husband for financial support. There are no financial expectations for the young woman if she is married: In fact, her husband may even forbid her from working. The age code in the quinceañera ritual conflicts with today's Mexican-American women's expectations of financial independence. Many state laws within the United States, moreover, forbid individuals under 18 to work full time or to be lawfully wed. These laws fit with the increasing expectation that the young Mexican-American woman will continue her education in order to become financially independent from her parents (and her eventual spouse). A realistic age for a contemporary quinceañera, therefore, might be eighteen or even twenty years of age.

SOCIAL CHANGES: CULTURAL DISASSOCIATION AND ACCULTURATION

Traditional rituals like the quinceañera are associated with sacred traditions of the Mexican culture. Young Mexican-American women in urban settings, however, no longer rely on this ritual to sustain a link to the past, and they decreasingly support a ritual that, in essence, is an open invitation for men from other extended families to begin courting her for marriage. This is a dramatic shift in the meaning of the quinceañera for women in the Mexican-American culture. Women are working toward new personal and social identities for themselves, separate from the Mexican social norm. This shift coincides with Williams's analysis of urbanization of Mexican-Americans.

What has been the catalyst for this shift? One Mexican-American woman whom I interviewed[3] was raised in El Paso, Texas. She stated that quinceañeras are occurring less and less frequently due to the education of women, the variety of social classes, financial resources, social norms, and religions that confront urban Mexican-Americans. The traditional sex-role expectation of Mexican-American women has changed to emphasize the creation of their own social identities that are separate from their fathers or husbands. Education and an occupation allow young Mexican-American women to create social identities that were unavailable to their mothers and grandmothers. This may be carried a step further by young Mexican-American women who decide whom to marry (including someone outside their own culture), when to marry, and when to start families. Young Mexican-American women thus distance themselves from the sex and age codes the ritual perpetuates. However, this disassociation also offers no opportunity to create communitas with extended family members and the community, thus continuing the decline of social memory of the quinceañera ritual.

Mexican-American women play an active role in the family structure, yet they are defined as subordinate to fathers and husbands within the family (a structure reinforced by the religious system). This pattern of women in the culture has had a tendency to create a sex code for women: A "good" woman marries, stays home, bears and rears children, and maintains the ideal family pattern. The challenge to this image are the young Mexican-American women who enter the public sector and decide when and to what extent they wish to participate in the traditional role of women in the culture. The new, different images create difficulties for interpreting the role of Mexican-American women in contemporary Mexican-American families and communities. As Williams (1990, 23) explains: "As [Mexican-American women] gain access to information, they gain social power. And as they gain social power, the old cultural structures change." This can be diagrammed as follows:

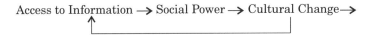

Access to Information → Social Power → Cultural Change→

"As [Mexican-American women] gain information, they are able to change their lives" (Blea 1992, 93).

Another woman whom I interviewed[4] said that she did not want her daughters (one in high school and others who previously attended universities) to go through the ritual process of women "going from one household to another." This woman viewed the ritual as a shamelessly glorified way to "expose the daughter to society" and as an "invitation to get the girl married." Many Mexican-American mothers did not go through the ritual, nor do their daughters, causing the ritual to fade from Mexican-American society and from succeeding generations of young Mexican-American women. This rejection creates a disassociation among and between generations and a distancing from the age and sex codes associated with them.

This change can be seen as part of "acculturation" and an outcome of assimilation and urbanization in the Mexican-American community. The concept "implies an acceptance of the minority and majority group. Over time the norms, values and behaviors of both groups are modified through contact" (Rotheram-Borus 1993, 87). Acculturation remains selective and problematic, nonetheless. For example, many young Mexican-American women recognize the pragmatic values of the new culture; however, they still respect and practice certain traditions of their own heritage: This is selective acculturation (Melville 1980, 149).

Examining my own experiences, my three sisters and I did not go through the quinceañera ritual because our modern perception was that it perpetuated the limited role of women in the Mexican culture. We still maintain core cultural values (such as the importance of family) but with a modern social perspective, that is, selective acculturation. In light of changing social norms, future generations will have less understanding of the quinceañera, the communitas it created, the core codes it perpetuated, and the origins of Mexican-American women's social identity and role.

CONCLUSION

The Mexican-American initiation ritual of young girls creates communitas and perpetuates traditional sex and age codes. Turner's concept of communitas defines the union created by the young woman and between her *corte de honor*, her extended family, other families, and the community during the liminal phase of the quinceañera ritual. The active use and continuation of Deegan's sex and age core codes are evident in this rite of passage from childhood to adulthood. The quinceañera ritual is a catalyst in the creation of communitas among the initiant, her family, and her community. Simultaneously, the sex and age core codes in the quinceañera ritual maintain the oppression and repression of women in the Mexican culture while alienating contemporary Mexican-American women who actively distance themselves from the ritual to create new social identities. Thus the perception of the quinceañera ritual by young Mexican-American women is changing in our contemporary social context, as reflected by Williams's theory of changing family structures in urbanized, Mexican-American families.

The sex and age codes ingrained in the quinceañera ritual cause it to become less and less practiced by young Mexican-American girls who refuse to participate in it as urbanization and their access to education increases. Death of the ritual leads to diminishment of the core codes in the ritual; however, it may also lead to a loss of communitas within that cultural community.

The weakening of this ritual would decrease what Deegan calls the "ritual echo" of the quinceañera, which refers to the reinforcing pattern of rituals to repeat similar rules and meaning across different antistructural situations. In American rituals, this echo sustains inequities within an alienated but partially satisfied community. Deegan (1989a, 153) notes that this echo can reflect an absence as well as a presence: "Rituals can, therefore, 'echo' an absence of women as well as their typical presence. Rituals augment, build, reinforce, and maintain inequity in a way that other forms of everyday life cannot." The fading of the quinceañera may open new, liberating opportunities for young Mexican-

American women as well as initiate a decline in communitas for the broader social group. If succeeding generations refuse to take part in a ritual that is centered on sex and age, the ritual echo will fade within the culture. Education, occupation, and the creation of new social identities for young Mexican-American women are influences that contribute to the fading ritual echo.

One way in which young Mexican-American women distance themselves from these codes and attain new social and cultural identities is through education. Young Mexican-American girls want to finish high school and continue with higher education. In my personal experience, I encouraged my parents to accompany me to university orientation and to visit me while I was at university. My father always refused; however, my mother (with no more than a fifth-grade education) accepted these invitations and was exposed to a world of possibilities she had never had. As Williams (1990, 93) notes, the "daughter who becomes better educated than the mother plays a role in socializing the latter." There is a desire to create a social identity, to meet the demands of everyday life and be independent; this is contrary to the roles of Mexican-American women from only a few decades ago. I would encourage further research on the effect of the contemporary social context on other women's rituals within the Mexican and Mexican-American communities not only in the United States, but also in Mexico and other Latin American counties.

There are beneficial claims that can be made for the quinceañera: It symbolically transforms the girl into a woman; it can claim to renew society by providing it with a new, productive member; and it can bring the social community together by generating communitas in a joyous celebration. The desired end is to make a girl ready and willing to assume the traditional place of a woman as defined within the Mexican culture (Bruce Lincoln 1981, 102–9). But can such a ritual "fit" in today's social context? Lankford (1994, 44) states in the text accompanying her pictorial of a quinceañera:

The sights and sounds of this evening were not just about Martha Jimenez [a young girl who just went through her quinceañera]; they were signs, symbols and songs of how young [Mexican-American women] move from their carefree girlhood into the choice-filled world of womanhood. . . . Through her quinceañera she has taken the first steps in a journey forward into womanhood and into the new life that has opened before her.

Lankford implies that the world is open to this young woman, a perspective that is not reflected in the sex and age core codes of the ritual. Perhaps this young woman will distance herself from the automatic early marriage and move toward today's social context of womanhood: educated and open to many opportunities that *may* include marriage and a family. It would be interesting to see Martha Jimenez again, but in five or twenty-five years from now.

NOTES

1. This is a good example of a participatory ritual and a media-constructed ritual occurring simultaneously.

2. I identify myself and those in similar cultural circumstances as "Mexican-American" to locate my cultural identity within the Latin-American cultural spectrum. Recently, there have been ongoing debates concerning identifying/labeling individuals with Mexican or Latin American ancestry (the same holds true for other cultures). I will not comment upon the other labels used to identify those with Mexican ancestry: Chicano/a, Latino/a, Hispanic, and so on. The choice of certain labels is a political decision, based upon ideology, and/or socioeconomic class status, regardless of generational status in the United States, Spanish-language usage, and/or practices of Mexican cultural traditions.

3. Interview on 5 March 1996 with a married Mexican-American woman who lives in a small midwestern city.

4. Interview on 2 March 1996 with a married Mexican-American woman who lives in a large western city.

Bibliography

UNPUBLISHED REFERENCES

Baron, Kate. 1989. "Strippers: The Undressing of an Occupation."
Andre Norton to Mary Jo Deegan, 14 February 1995, pp. 1–2.
Debra Deitering to Lisa K. Nielsen, personal communication, circa 1996.
Disney University. Training manual distributed to Disney employees at Disney-
    land Paris.

PUBLISHED REFERENCES

Addams, Jane. 1910. *Twenty Years at Hull-House*. New York: Macmillan.
———. 1930a. *The Second Twenty Years at Hull-House*. New York: Macmillan.
———. 1930b. "The Play Instinct and the Arts." *Religious Education* 25 (No-
    vember): 808–19.
Aho, James. 1994. *This Thing of Darkness: A Sociology of the Enemy*. Seattle:
    University of Washington.
Allport, Gordon W. 1954. *The Nature of Prejudice*. Reading, Mass.: Addison-
    Wesley.
Altman, Yochanan. 1995. "A Theme Park in a Cultural Straitjacket." *Managing
    Leisure* 1 (1): 43–56.
———. 1997. "The High Flying, Fast Trading Anglo-Saxon Executive." *Career
    Development International* 2 (7): n.p.
Altman, Yochanan, and J. Billsberry. 1994. "An Awareness of International
    Culture Understanding Structures and Cultures." Appendix in *The
    Capable Manager*. Milton Keynes, UK: Open University.

Altman, Yochanan, and Tracy Jones. 1992. "Euro Disney—First Reflections on an American Cultural Concept in a European Environment." Paper presented at the Americanization of Culture Conference: Swansea, Wales, September.

———. 1993. "Euro Disney: The Magic Is Missing." *Crossborder* 1: 18–20.

Anderson, Leon, and Thomas C. Calhoun. 1992. "Facilitative Aspects of Field Research with Deviant Street Populations." *Sociological Inquiry* 62 (Fall): 490–98.

Anderson, Leon, and Mara Holt. 1990. "Teaching Writing in Sociology: A Social Constructionist Approach." *Teaching Sociology* 18 (April): 179–84.

Anti-Defamation League. 1996. Text of ADL research report "Poisoning the Airwaves: The Extremist Message of Hate on Shortwave Radio." *U.S. Newswire* (February 1).

Ball, Michael R. 1990. *Professional Wrestling as Ritual Drama in American Popular Culture*. Lewiston, New York: Mellen.

Baudrillard, Jean. 1988. *America*. London, UK: Verso.

Baum, L. Frank. 1902. *The Life and Adventures of Santa Claus*. Indianapolis: Bowen-Merrill.

———. 1909. *The Road to Oz*. Chicago: Reilly and Lee.

Becker, Howard S. 1986. *Writing for Social Scientists: How to Start and Finish Your Thesis, Book, or Article*. Chicago: University of Chicago Press.

Belk, Russell W. 1987. "A Child's Christmas in America: Santa Claus as Deity, Consumption as Religion." *Journal of American Culture* 10 (Spring): 87–100.

Bell, Ella Louise. 1992. "Myths, Stereotypes, and Realities of Black Women: A Personal Reflection." *Journal of Applied Behavioral Science* 28 (September): 363–76.

Bellah, Robert. 1970. *Beyond Belief*. New York: Harper & Row.

Bendiksen, Robert. 1994. "The Sociology of Death," pp. 59–81 in *Death and Identity*. Edited by Robert Fulton and Robert Bendiksen. Bowie, Md.: Charles.

Benjamin, Ludy. 1995. "The Santa Claus Survey: A Pioneering Nebraska Study in Child Psychology." *Nebraska History* 76 (Winter): 188–94.

Berger, Peter L., Bridgette Berger, and Hans Kellner. 1973. *The Homeless Mind*. New York: Vintage.

Berger, Peter L., and Hans Kellner. 1970. "Marriage and the Construction of Reality," pp. 49–72 in *Recent Sociology*. Edited by Hans Peter Dreitzel. New York: Macmillan.

Berger, Peter, and Thomas Luckmann. 1966. *The Social Construction of Reality*. Garden City, N.Y.: Doubleday.

Besson, Virginia. 1996. "E-F (Enterprises-Formation) Mickey Retrouve le Sourire." *Strategies d'Enterprise*, no. 91 (April): 10–13.

Blackwood, A. 1942. *The Funeral: A Source Book for Ministers*. Philadelphia: Westminister.

Blasi, Anthony J. 1994. "Power, Class, Law: The Complementarity of Realpolitik and Soft Sociologies." *Sociologia Internationalis* 32 (1): 47–54.

Blauner, Robert. 1994. "Death and the Social Structure," pp. 35–58 in *Death and Identity*. Edited by Robert Fulton and Robert Bendiksen. Bowie, Md.: Charles.

Blea, Irene I. 1992. *La Chicana and the Intersection of Race, Class, and Gender*. New York: Praeger.

Bloch, Robert, and Andre Norton. 1990. *The Jekyll Legacy*. New York: TOR.

Blumer, Herbert. 1969. *Symbolic Interactionism: Perspective and Method*. Englewood Cliffs, N.J.: Prentice-Hall.

Boles, J., and A. P. Garbin. 1974. "The Strip Club and Customer-Stripper Patterns of Interaction." *Sociology and Social Research* 58 (January): 136–44.

Boorstin, Daniel. 1992. *The Image: A Guide to Pseudo-events in America*. New York: Vintage.

Borcover, Alfred. 1992. "Grumps Needn't Apply: For Disney 'Cast' It's Always Showtime." *Chicago Tribune* (7 June), section 12, p. 2, cols. 1–4.

Bowman, LeRoy Edward. 1973. *The American Funeral: A Study in Guilt, Extravagance, and Sublimity*. Westport, Conn.: Greenwood.

Bradley, Marion Zimmer, Julian May, and Andre Norton. 1990. *Black Trillium*. New York: Doubleday.

Bregman, Lucy, and Sara Thiermann. 1995. *First Person Mortal: Personal Narratives of Dying, Death, and Grief*. New York: Paragon House.

Buck, Genevieve. 1995. "Sweatshop Labor: An Issue Most Retailers Prefer to Keep in the Closet." *Chicago Tribune* (10 December).

Calhoun, Thomas. 1992. "Male Street Hustling: Introduction Processes and Stigma Containment." *Sociological Spectrum* 12 (January): 35–52.

Carey, Sandra Harley, Robert A. Peterson, and Louis K. Sharpe. 1974. "A Study of Recruitment and Socialization into Two Deviant Occupations." *Sociological Symposium* 11 (Spring): 11–24.

Cawelti, John G. 1969. "The Concept of Formula in the Study of Popular Literature." *Journal of Popular Culture* 3 (Winter): 381–90.

Chapple, Eliot D., and Carleton S. Coon. 1942. *Principles of Anthropology*. New York: Henry Holt.

Cherlin, Andrew. 1978. "Remarriage as an Incomplete Institution." *American Journal of Sociology* 84 (November): 634–50.

———. 1992. *Marriage, Divorce, Remarriage*. Cambridge: Harvard University.

Chicago Commission on Race Relations. 1922. *The Negro in Chicago*. Chicago: University of Chicago Press.

Christian Posse Comitatus. 1996. *The Watchman*. (Spring).

Christianson, Richard. 1997. "Hey Big Boy! I Want to Go to Disney World." *Chicago Tribune* (16 February): section 7, p. 1, col. 1.

Chutkow, Paul. 1992. "Who Will Control the Soul of French Cinema?" *New York Times* (9 August): section 2, p. 22, cols. 1–5.

Clendinnen, Inga. 1991. *Aztecs: An Interpretation*. New York: Cambridge University.

Coker, Frances H., and Allen Scarboro. 1990. "Writing to Learn in Upper-Division Sociology Courses: Two Case Studies." *Teaching Sociology* 18: 218–22.

Cooper, James, and Kathleen Madigan. 1994. "Business Outlook: At This Rate Santa's Elves Will Be Working Overtime." *Business Week* 3403 (12 December): 33–34.

———. 1995. "Business Outlook: A Chorus of 'Humbug' This Holiday Season." *Business Week* 3452 (27 November): 33–34.

Czikzentmihalyi, Mihaly. 1975. *Beyond Boredom and Anxiety.* San Francisco: Jossey-Bass.

Darrow, Clarence. 1932. *The Story of My Life.* New York: Grossett and Dunlap.

Davis, Allen F. 1973. *American Heroine.* New York: Oxford University.

Deegan, Mary Jo. 1978. "Women in Sociology, 1890–1930." *Journal of the History of Sociology* 1 (Fall): 11–34.

———. 1981. "Early Women Sociologists and the American Sociological Society: Patterns of Inclusion and Exclusion." *American Sociologist* 16 (February): 14–24.

———. 1986a. "Holidays as Multiple Realities: Experiencing Good Times and Bad Times After a Disabling Injury." *Journal of Sociology and Social Welfare* 13 (December): 786–803.

———. 1986b. "The Clinical Sociology of Jessie Taft." *Clinical Sociology Review* 4: 33–45.

———. 1987a. "An American Dream: The Historical Connections Between Women, Humanism, and Sociology, 1890–1920." *Humanity and Society* 11 (August): 353–65.

———. 1987b. "Working Hypotheses for Women and Social Change," pp. 443–49 in *Women and Symbolic Interaction.* Edited by Mary Jo Deegan and Michael R. Hill. Boston: Allen and Unwin.

———. 1988a. *Jane Addams and the Men of the Chicago School, 1892 to 1918.* New Brunswick, N.J.: Transaction.

———. 1988b. "Transcending a Patriarchal Past: Teaching the History of Women in Sociology." *Teaching Sociology* 16 (April): 141–50.

———. 1988c. "W. E. B. DuBois and the Women of Hull-House." *American Sociologist* 19 (Winter): 301–11.

———. 1989a. *American Ritual Dramas: Social Rules and Cultural Meanings.* (Contributions in Sociology, No. 76). Westport, Conn.: Greenwood.

———. 1989b. "Sociology and Conviviality: A Conversation with Ellenhorn on Convivial Sociology." *Humanity and Society* 13 (February): 85–88.

———. 1989b. "*American Charities* as the Herald to a New Age," pp. ix–xxviii in *American Charities* by Amos G. Warner, print of 1894 text. New Brunswick, N.J.: Transaction.

———. 1992. "The Genesis of the International Self: Working Hypotheses Emerging from the Chicago Experience (1892–1918)," pp. 339–53 in *Non-European Youth and the Process of Immigration: For a Tolerant Society.* Edited by Luigi Tomasi. Trento, Italy: University of Trento and Trento Province.

———. 1993. "Consciousness-Raising in the USA: The Personal Is Political and the Political Is Personal." Paper presented at the International Interdisciplinary Congress of Women. San Jose, Costa Rica.

———. 1995a. "The Second Sex and the Chicago School: Women's Accounts, Knowledge, and Work, 1945–1960," pp. 322–64 in *A Second Chicago*

School?: The Development of a Postwar American Sociology. Edited by Gary Alan Fine. Chicago University of Chicago Press.

———. 1995b. "*The Year of the Unicorn* by Andre Norton," pp. 2572–76 in *Masterplots*. Edited by Frank N. Magill. Pasadena, CA: Salem Press.

———. 1996. "*Moon of Three Rings* by Andre Norton," pp. 641–42 in *Magill's Guide to Science Fiction and Fantasy Literature*. Edited by Frank N. Magill. Pasadena, CA: Salem Press.

———. 1997. "Gilman's Sociological Journey from *Herland* to *Ourland*," pp. 1–57 in *With Her In Ourland: Sequel to Herland*, by Charlotte Perkins Gilman. Westport, Conn.: Greenwood.

———, ed. 1991. *Women in Sociology: A Bio-Bibliographical Sourcebook*. Westport Conn.: Greenwood.

Deegan, Mary Jo, and Nancy A. Brooks, eds. 1985. *Women and Disability: The Double Handicap*. New Brunswick, N.J.: Transaction.

Deegan, Mary Jo, and Michael R. Hill. 1988. "We're Partners—Not Husband and Wife," pp. 246–47 in *Marriage and Families: Making Choices and Facing Change*, 3rd ed., by Mary Ann Lamanna and Agnes Reidmann. Belmont, Calif.: Wadsworth.

———. 1989. "The Presentation of the City on Fat-Letter Postcards," pp. 91–105 in *American Ritual Dramas: Social Rules and Cultural Meanings*, by Mary Jo Deegan. Westport, Conn.: Greenwood.

Deegan, Mary Jo, and Michael R. Hill, eds. 1987. *Women and Symbolic Interaction*. Boston: Allen and Unwin.

———. 1991. "Doctoral Dissertations as Liminal Journeys of the Self: Betwixt and Between in Graduate Sociology Programs." *Teaching Sociology* 19 (July): 322–32.

Deegan, Mary Jo, and Michael Stein. 1978. "Pornography as a Strip and a Frame." *Sociological Symposium* 20 (Fall): 27–44.

DeFord, Frank. 1971. *There She Is: The Life and Times of Miss America*. New York: Viking.

Deitering, Debra. 1994. *Anyone Can Be Miss America! The Propagandizing of the Miss America Pageant*. Houston: University of Houston.

Derber, Charles. 1996. *The Wilding of America*. New York: St. Martin's.

DeVries, S. J. 1964. "Evil," p. 182 in *The Interpreter's Dictionary of the Bible*. Edited by George Arthur Buttrick. New York: Abingdon.

Diggins, John Patrick. 1994. *The Promise of Pragmatism*. Chicago: University of Chicago Press.

"Disneyland Paris." 1995. *Capital* (February): 39–42.

"Divorced People Get Help Erasing Their Ex." 1996. *Chicago Tribune* (4 February): section 5, p. 7, cols. 1–5.

Doka, Kenneth J. 1989. *Disenfranchised Grief: Recognizing Hidden Sorrow*. Lexington, Mass.: Lexington.

Dressel, Paula, and David Peterson. 1982a. "Becoming a Male Stripper." *Work and Occupations* 8 (August): 387–406.

———. 1982b. "Gender Roles, Sexuality, and the Male Strip Show: The Structuring of Sexual Opportunity." *Sociological Focus* 15 (April): 151–62.

Dumont, R. G., and D. C. Foss. 1972. *The American View of Death: Acceptance or Denial?* Cambridge, Mass.: Schenkman.

Durkheim, Emile. 1915. *The Elementary Forms of the Religious Life*. Translated by George Swain. London, UK: George Allen and Unwin.

Elias, Norbert, and Eric Dunning. 1986. "The Quest for Excitement in Leisure," pp. 63–90 in *The Quest for Excitement*. Edited by Norbert Elias and Eric Dunning. Oxford, UK: Blackwell.

Enck, Graves E., and James D. Preston. 1988. "Counterfeit Intimacy: A Dramaturgical Analysis of an Erotic Performance." *Deviant Behavior* 9 (October-December): 369–81.

"Farmers Protest at Euro Disneyland." 1992. *Chicago Tribune* (27 June): section 1, p. 3, cols. 1–3.

Farrell, John C. 1967. *Beloved Lady*. Baltimore, Md.: Johns Hopkins University Press.

Feagin, Joseph R. 1992. "On Not Taking Gendered Racism Seriously: The Failure of the Mass Media and the Social Sciences." *Journal of Applied Behavioral Science* 28 (3): 400–406.

Fjellman, Stephen M. 1992. *Vynil Leaves*. Boulder, Colo.: Westview.

Franklin, Stephen. 1996. "An Economy Disconnected." *Chicago Tribune* (3 January): p. 1, cols. 2–6; p. 9, cols. 1–4.

Frideres, James. 1973. "Advertising, Buying Patterns and Children." *Journal of Advertising Research* 13 (1): 34–36.

Garfinkel, Harold. 1963. "A Conception of, and Experiments with, 'Trust' as a Condition of Stable Concerted Actions," pp. 184–92 in *Motivation and Social Interaction*. Edited by O. J. Harvey. New York: Ronald.

Giddens, Anthony. 1987. *Sociology: A Brief But Critical Introduction*. 2d ed. San Diego, Calif.: Harcourt, Brace, Jovanovich.

———. 1990. *The Consequences of Modernity*. Stanford, Calif.: Stanford University.

Gilbert, Margaret. 1989. *On Social Facts*. London, UK: Routledge.

Gilman, Charlotte Perkins. 1966/1898. *Women and Economics*. New York: Harper.

Glaser, Barney G., and Anselm L. Strauss. 1965. *Awareness of Dying*. Chicago: Aldine.

Goffman, Erving. 1959. *The Presentation of Self in Everyday Life*. Garden City, N.Y.: Doubleday.

———. 1961. *Asylums*. Garden City, N.Y.: Doubleday.

———. 1963. *Behavior in Public Places: Notes on the Social Organization of Gatherings*. New York: Harper & Row.

———. 1967. *Interaction Ritual: Essays on Face-to-Face Behavior*. New York: Harper & Row.

———. 1974. *Frame Analysis: An Essay on the Organization of Experience*. New York: Harper & Row.

———. 1979/1976. *Gender Advertisements*. Cambridge: Harvard University.

———. 1987. "The Arrangement Between the Sexes," pp. 51–78 in *Women and Symbolic Interaction*. Edited by Mary Jo Deegan and Michael R. Hill. Boston: Allen and Unwin.

Gorer, Geoffrey. 1948. *The Americans*. London, UK: Cresset.

———. 1960. "The Pornography of Death," pp. 402–407 in *Identity and Anxiety: Survival of the Person in Mass Society*. Edited by M. Stein, A. Vidich, and D. White. New York: Free Press.

———. 1977. *Death, Grief, and Mourning*. Garden City, N.Y.: Doubleday.

Grover, Ron. 1991. *The Disney Touch*. Homewood, Ill.: Business One.

Habermas, Jurgen. 1987. *The Theory of Communicative Action*, vol. 2. Translated by Thomas McCarthy. Boston: Beacon.

Haines, David. 1988. "Ritual or Ritual?: Dinnertime and Christmas Among Some Ordinary American Families." *Semiotica* 68 (1/2): 75–88.

Hammond, Phillip E., ed. 1964. *Sociologists at Work: Essays on the Craft of Social Research*. New York: Basic Books.

Heller, Zoe. 1995. "The Zoe Heller Column." *Sunday Times Magazine* (5 November): 32.

Hill, Michael R. 1981. "Tourism, Authenticity, and Cuba." *SWS [Sociologists for Women in Society] Network* 12(1): 8, 19.

———. 1983. "Changes in the Status of Cuban Women Since the Revolution: Some Comments on a Study Tour in Cuba." *Transition: Quarterly Journal of the Socially and Ecologically Responsible Geographers* 13(1): 2–8.

———. 1987. "Novels, Thought Experiments, and Humanist Sociology in the Classroom: Mari Sandoz and *Capital City*." *Teaching Sociology* 15 (January): 38–44.

———. 1989. "Empiricism and Reason in Harriet Martineau's Sociology," pp. xv–lx in *How to Observe Morals and Manners*, by Harriet Martineau. New Brunswick, N.J.: Transaction.

Hofstede, Geert H. 1980. *Culture's Consequences: International Differences in Work-Related Values*. Beverly Hills, Calif.: Sage.

———. 1991. *Cultures and Organization: Software of the Mind*. New York: McGraw-Hill.

Horowitz, Ruth. 1987. "Passion, Submission, and Motherhood," pp. 251–74 in *Women and Symbolic Interaction*. Edited by Mary Jo Deegan and Michael R. Hill. Boston: Allen & Unwin.

Johnson, Colleen L. 1988. *Ex-Familia: Grandparents, Parents, and Children Adjust to Divorce*. New Brunswick, N.J.: Rutgers University.

Johnson, K. A. 1991. "Objective News and Other Myths: The Poisoning of Young Black Minds." *Journal of Negro Education* 60 (Summer): 328–41.

Johnston, Christopher. 1996. "IHT [International Herald Tribune] Sega Tests the Theme-Park Route." *International Manager* (12 September): 12.

Kammerman, Jack B. 1988. *Death in the Midst of Life: Social and Cultural Influences on Death, Grief, and Mourning*. Englewood Cliffs, N.J.: Prentice-Hall.

Kanter, Rosabeth Moss. 1977. *Men and Women of the Corporation*. New York: Basic.

Kübler-Ross, Elizabeth. 1969. *On Death and Dying*. New York: Macmillan.

La Fontaine, J. S. 1985. *Initiation: Ritual Drama and Secret Knowledge Across the World*. Harmondsworth, UK: Penguin.

Lankford, Mary D. 1994. *Quinceañera: A Latina's Journey to Womanhood.* Brookfield, Conn.: Millbrook.

"Late Rush of Shoppers Can't Cheer Retailers: End-of-Season Sales Bring in Customers, But Markdowns Expected to Wipe Out Profit." 1995. *Chicago Tribune* (25 December): p. 6, cols. 5–6.

Lincoln, Bruce. 1981. *Emerging from the Chrysalis: Studies in Rituals of Women's Initiation.* Cambridge: Harvard University Press.

Lincoln, C. Eric, and Lawrence H. Mamiya. 1990. *The Black Church in the African American Experience.* Durham, N.C.: Duke University Press.

Luckmann, Thomas. 1967. *The Invisible Religion: The Problem of Religion in Modern Society.* New York: Macmillan.

McCaghy, Charles, and James K. Skipper. 1969. "Lesbian Behavior as an Adaptation to the Occupation of Stripping." *Social Problems* 17 (Fall): 262–70.

———. 1972. "Stripping: Anatomy of a Deviant Life Style," pp. 362–73 in *Life Styles: Diversity in American Society.* Edited by Saul D. Feldman and G. W. Thielbar. Boston: Little, Brown.

Mandelbaum, D. G. 1994. "Social Uses of Funeral Rites," pp. 344–62 in *Death and Identity.* Edited by Robert Fulton and Robert Bendiksen. Bowie, Md.: Charles.

Margolis, Maxine L., and Marigene Arnold. 1993. "Turning the Tables?: Male Strippers and the Gender Hierarchy in America," pp. 334–50 in *Sex and Gender Hierarchies.* Edited by Barbara Diane Miller. Cambridge, UK: Cambridge University Press.

Marlière, O. 1992. "Le Futuroscope est-il un Resort?" *Cahiers d'Espaces* (27 June): n.p.

Marshall, George N. 1981. *Facing Death and Grief: A Sensible Perspective for the Modern Person.* Buffalo, N.Y.: Prometheus Books.

Martin, Joel W., and Conrad E. Ostwalt, Jr., eds. 1995. *Screening the Sacred: Religion, Myth, and Ideology in Popular American Film.* Boulder, Colo.: Westview.

Martindale, Don, and Raj P. Mohan, eds. 1980. *Ideas and Realities: Some Problem Areas of Professional Social Science.* Ghaziabad, India: Intercontinental.

Marx, Karl. 1967/1843. "Toward the Critique of Hegel's Philosophy of Law: Introduction," pp. 249–64 in *Writings of the Young Marx on Philosophy and Society.* Edited by Lloyd D. Easton and Kurt H. Guddat. Garden City, N.Y.: Anchor Doubleday.

———. 1975. *Theories of Surplus-Value.* Moscow, USSR: Progress Publishers.

Mead, George H. 1899. "The Working Hypothesis in Social Reform." *American Journal of Sociology* 5 (November): 367–71.

———. 1934. *Mind, Self and Society from the Standpoint of a Social Behaviorist.* Edited by Charles Morris. Chicago: University of Chicago Press.

Merton, Robert. 1949. *Social Structure.* New York: Free Press.

Messner, Steven F., and Richard Rosenfeld. 1994. *Crime and the American Dream.* Belmont, Calif.: Wadsworth.

Melville, Margarita B. 1980. *Twice a Minority: Mexican American Women.* St. Louis: Mosby.

Mills, C. Wright. 1956. *The Power Elite*. New York: Oxford University Press.

Mirande, Alfredo. 1985. *The Chicano Experience: An Alternative Perspective*. Notre Dame, Ind.: University of Notre Dame.

Mitford, Jessica. 1963. *The American Way of Death*. New York: Simon & Schuster.

Moore, Clement. 1844. *Poems by Clement C. Moore*. New York: Barttell & Walford.

Mullen, Ken. 1985. "The Impure Performance Frame of the Public House Entertainer." *Urban Life* 14 (July): 181–203.

Natanson, Maurice. 1970. *The Journeying Self: A Study in Philosophy and Social Role*. Reading, Mass.: Addison-Wesley.

Norton, Andre. 1963. *Witch World*. New York: Ace.

———. 1964. *Web of the Witch World*. New York: Ace.

———. 1965a. *The Year of the Unicorn*. New York: Ace.

———. 1965b. *Three Against the Witch World*. New York: Ace.

———. 1967. *Warlock of the Witch World*. New York: Ace.

———. 1968. *Sorceresses of the Witch World*. New York: Ace.

———. 1972a. *Spell of the Witch World*. New York: DAW.

———. 1972b. *The Crystal Gryphon*. New York: DAW.

———. 1975. *The Book of Andre Norton*. Edited by Roger Elwood. New York: DAW.

———. 1981. *Horn Crown*. New York: DAW.

Norton, Andre, ed. 1987. *Tales of the Witch World*, vol. 1. New York: TOR.

———. 1989. *Tales of the Witch World*, vol. 2. New York: TOR.

———. 1990. *Tales of the Witch World*, vol. 3. New York: TOR.

Norton, Andre, and Robert Adams, eds. 1985. *Magic in Ithkar*. New York: TOR.

Norton, Andre, and A. C. Crispin. 1984. *Gryphon's Eyrie*. New York: TOR.

Norton, Andre, and Lyn McConachie. 1995. *Keys of the Keplian*. New York: Warner.

Norton, Andre, with Pamela M. Griffen. 1991. *Storms of Victory: Witch World: The Turning*. New York: TOR.

Norton, Andre, with Pamela M. Griffen and Mary H. Schaub. 1992. *Flight of Vengeance: The Turning, Book 2*. New York: TOR.

Norton, Andre, and Mercedes Lackey. 1991. *The Elvenbane: An Epic High Fantasy of the Halfblood Chronicles*. New York: TOR.

Ogintz, Eileen. 1992. "Tips: A Disney Dozen." *Chicago Tribune* (14 June): section 12, p. 8, cols 5–6; p. 9, cols. 1–4.

Parsons, Talcott, and Victor Lidz. 1967. "Death in American Society," pp. 133–70 in *Essays in Self-Destruction*. Edited by E. Schneidman. New York: Science House.

Pattison, E. Mansell. 1977. *The Experience of Dying*. Englewood Cliffs, N.J.: Prentice-Hall.

Peretti, Peter O., and Patrick O'Connor. 1989. "Effects of Incongruence Between the Perceived Self and the Ideal Self on Emotional Stability of Stripteasers." *Social Behavior and Personality* 17 (Fall): 81–92.

Persons, Stow. 1987. *Ethnic Studies at Chicago, 1905–45*. Urbana, Ill.: University of Illinois.

Peterson, David, and Paula Dressel. 1982. "Equal Time for Women." *Urban Life* 11 (July): 185–208.

Pierce, William [Andrew Macdonald]. 1980/1978. *The Turner Diaries*. Hillsboro, W.Va.: National Vanguard Books.

Piliavin, Jane Allyn. 1989. " 'When in Doubt, Ask the Subject': A Response to Egan." *Teaching Sociology* 17: 208–11

Pine, V. R. 1975. *Caretaker of the Dead: The American Funeral Director*. New York: Irvington.

Pollack, Andrew. 1992. "Export News: 'Twin Peaks' Mania Peaks in Japan." *New York Times* (2 August): section 2, p. 16, cols. 1–5.

Pretes, Michael. 1995. "Postmodern Tourism: The Santa Claus Industry." *Annals of Tourism Research* 22 (1): 1–15.

Price-Bonham, Sharon, and J. Balswick. 1980. "The Noninstitutions: Divorce, Desertion, and Remarriage." *Journal of Marriage and the Family* 42 (November): 959–72.

Project on Disney. 1995. *Inside the Mouse*. Durham, N.C.: Duke University Press.

Redfield, Robert. 1962. "Social Science among the Humanities," pp. 43–57 in *Human Nature and the Study of Society. The Papers of Robert Redfield, Volume I*. Edited by Margaret Park Redfield. Chicago: University of Chicago Press.

Reid, Scott A., Jonathon A. Epstein, and D. E. Benson. 1994a. "Does Exotic Dancing Pay Well But Cost Dearly?" pp. 284–88 in *Readings in Deviance*. Edited by Alex Thio and Thomas C. Calhoun. New York: Harper Collins.

———. 1994b. "Role Identity in a Devalued Occupation: The Case of Female Exotic Dancers." *Sociological Focus* 27 (February): 1–17.

Reinhardt, Dietrich. n.d. "Sword of Truth." *The Realm Reporter* (January, February, March).

Reinharz, Shulamit. 1983. "Experiential Analysis: A Contribution to Feminist Research," pp. 162–91 in *Theories of Women's Studies*. Edited by Gloria Bowles. Boston: Routledge and Kegan Paul.

———. 1984. *On Becoming a Social Scientist*, with a new introduction by Shulamit Reinharz. New Brunswick, N.J.: Transaction.

Residents of Hull-House. 1895. *Hull-House Maps and Papers*. New York: Crowell.

Richards, Pamela. 1986. "Risk," pp. 108–20 in *Writing for Social Scientists*, by Howard S. Becker, with a chapter by Pamela Richards. Chicago: University of Chicago Press.

Ricoeur, Paul. 1969. *The Symbolism of Evil*. Boston, MA: Beacon.

Riedmann, Agnes. 1988. "Ex-Wife at the Funeral: Keyed Anti-Structure." *Free Inquiry in Creative Sociology* 16 (May): 123–29.

Riley, Matilda White, ed. 1988. *Sociological Lives*. Newbury Park, Calif.: Sage.

Risman, Barbara. 1987. "College Women and Sororities: The Social Construction and Reaffirmation of Gender Roles," pp. 125–40 in *Women and Symbolic Interaction*. Edited by Mary Jo Deegan and Michael R. Hill. Boston: Allen and Unwin.

Riverol, A. R. 1992. *Live From Atlantic City—A History of the Miss America Pageant.* Bowling Green, Ohio: Bowling Green University.

Ronai, Carol R., and Carolyn Ellis. 1989. "Turn-ons for Money: Interactional Strategies of the Table Dancer." *Journal of Contemporary Ethnography* 18 (October): 271–98.

Rosenberg, Rosalind. 1982. *Beyond Separate Spheres.* New Haven: Yale University Press.

Rossiter, Margaret. 1982. *Women Scientists in America.* Baltimore, Md: Johns Hopkins University Press.

Rotheram-Borus, Mary Jane. 1993. "Biculturalism Among Adolescents," pp. 81–104 in *Ethnic Identity: Formation and Transmission among Hispanics and Other Minorities.* Edited by Martha E. Bernal and George P. Knight. New York: State University of New York.

Rowley, Storer H. 1993. "In Canada, Santa Has a Special Place." *Chicago Tribune* (24 December): p. 6, cols. 1–4.

Salva-Ramirez, Mary-Angie. 1995. "McDonald's: A Prime Example of Corporate Culture." *Public Relations Quarterly* 40 (Winter): 30–33.

Samuels, Gary. 1996. "Golden Arches Galore." *Forbes* 158 (4 November): 46–49.

Schlobin, Roger C. 1993. "The Formulaic and Rites of Transformation in Andre Norton's 'Magic' Series," pp. 37–457 in *Science Fiction and the Young Reader.* Edited by C. W. Sullivan, III. Westport, Conn.: Greenwood Press, 1993.

———. 1994. "Andre Norton: The Author Becomes Her Fiction and Creates Life," pp. 172–77 in *Science Fiction and Fantasy Book Review Annual 1991.* Edited by Robert A. Collins and Robert Latham. Westport, Conn.: Greenwood Press.

Schlobin, Roger C., and Irene R. Harrison. 1995. Andre Norton: A Primary and Secondary Bibliography. Framingham, Mass.: NESFA.

Schneider, David M. 1968. *American Kinship: A Cultural Account.* Englewood Cliffs, N.J.: Prentice-Hall.

Schneider, Keith. 1995. "Hate Groups Use Tools of the Electronic Trade." *New York Times* (March 13): L, A12.

Schroer, Todd J. 1993. *The Role of Music in the Formation and Maintenance of the DeadHead and Skinhead Countercultures.* M.A. thesis, Department of Sociology, University of California-Santa Barbara.

———. 1996. "Media Representations, Cognitive Schemas, and Their Effects." Paper presented at the Midwest Sociological Society Meetings, Chicago.

Schutz, Alfred. 1967. *The Phenomenology of The Social World.* Translated by George Walsh and Frederick Lehnert. Introduction by George Walsh. Evanston, Ill.: Northwestern University.

———. 1971. *Collected Papers, I: The Problem of Social Reality.* Edited by Maurice Natanson. The Hague, The Netherlands: Martinus Nijhoff.

Schwartz, Susan. 1985. *Moonsinger's Friends: An Anthology in Honor of Andre Norton.* New York: Bluejay Books.

Siegfreid, Charlene Haddock. 1991. "Where Are All the Feminist Pragmatists?" *Hypatia* 6 (Summer): 1–20.

Skipper, James K., and Charles H. McCaghy. 1970. "Stripteasers: The Anatomy and Career Contingencies of a Deviant Occupation." *Social Problems* 17 (Winter): 391–405.

Smith, Dennis. 1988. *The Chicago School: A Liberal Critique of Capitalism.* New York: Macmillan.

Smith, Dorothy E. 1974a. "The Ideological Practice of Sociology." *Catalyst* 8 (Winter): 39–54.

———. 1974b. "Women's Perspective as a Radical Critique of Sociology." *Sociological Inquiry* 4 (1): 7–13.

———. 1975 "An Analysis of Ideological Structures and How Women are Excluded." *Canadian Review of Sociology and Anthropology 12*, part 1: 353–69.

———. 1977a. *Feminism and Marxism—A Place to Begin, A Way To Go.* Vancouver, B.C., Canada: New Star Books.

———. 1977b. "Some Implications of a Sociology for Women," pp. 15–29 in *Woman in a Man-Made World*, 2d ed. Edited by Nona Glazer and Helen Youngelson Waeher. Chicago: Rand McNally.

———. 1987. *The Everyday World As Problematic: A Feminist Sociology.* Boston: Northeastern University.

———. 1988. "The Deep Structure of Gender Antithesis: Another View of Capitalism and Patriarchy," pp. 23–36 in *A Feminist Ethic for Social Science Research.* Edited by the Nebraska Sociological Feminist Collective. Lewiston, N.Y.: Edwin Mellen.

Snow, David E., and Robert D. Benford. 1988. "Ideology, Frame Resonance and Participant Mobilization." *International Social Movement Research* 1: 197–217.

Sorkin, Michael, ed. 1992. *Variations on a Theme Park.* New York: Noonday.

Spear, Allen H. 1967. *Black Chicago: The Making of a Negro Ghetto, 1890–1920.* Chicago: University of Chicago Press.

Spender, Dale. 1983. *Feminist Theorists: Three Centuries of Key Women Thinkers.* New York: Pantheon.

———. 1988. *Women of Ideas (and What Men Have Done to Them): From Aphra Behn to Adrienne Rich.* Boston: Pandora.

SPLC [Southern Poverty Law Center]. 1996. "National Alliance: North America's Largest Neo-Nazi Group Flourishing." *Intelligence Report* (May): 5–8.

———. 1996. "Online Allies." *False Patriots: The Threat of Antigovernment Extremists.* Montgomery, Ala.: Southern Poverty Law Center.

Stacey, Judith. 1990. *Brave New Families: Stories of Domestic Upheaval in the Late Twentieth Century.* New York: Basic Books.

Stanton, Alfred H., and Morris S. Schwartz. 1954. *The Mental Hospital.* New York: Basic Books.

Stivers, Richard. 1982. *Evil in Modern Myth and Ritual.* Athens: The University of Georgia Press.

Stone, Gregory P. 1959. "Clothing and Social Relations: A Study of Appearance in the Context of Community Life." Ph.D. dissertation, Department of Sociology, University of Chicago.

Stone, Irving. 1941. *Clarence Darrow for the Defense*. Garden City, N.J.: Doubleday, Doran.

Street, Arthur L. H. 1924. *American Funeral Law: A Manual of Law Affecting Funeral Directors and Embalmers*. Chicago: Trade Periodical Co.

Sudnow, David. 1967. *Passing On*. Englewood Cliffs, N.J.: Prentice-Hall.

Sylvan, David J., and Barry Glassner. 1985. *A Rationalist Methodology for the Social Sciences*. Oxford, UK: Blackwell.

Taft, Jessie. 1915. *The Woman Movement from the Point of View of Social Consciousness*. Chicago: University of Chicago Press.

———. 1942. "The Function of the Personality Course in the Practice Unit," pp. 55–74 in *Training for Skill in Social Case Work*. Edited by Virgina P. Robinson. Philadelphia: University of Pennsylvania.

———. 1962. *Jessie Taft: Therapist and Social Work Educator*. Edited by Virginia Robinson. Philadelphia: University of Pennsylvania.

Talbot, Marion. 1936. *More Than Lore*. Chicago: University of Chicago Press.

Talbot, Marion, and Lois Kimball Mathews Rosenberry. 1931. *The History of the American Association of University Women*. Cambridge, Mass.: Houghton Mifflin.

Thompson, William E., and Jackie L. Harred. 1992. "Topless Dancers: Managing Stigma in a Deviant Occupation." *Deviant Behavior* 13 (July–September): 291–311.

Tobias, Patricia Eliot. 1996. "Christmas in Oz." *The Baum Bugle* 40 (Fall): 22–29.

Tugend, Tom. 1994. "As Hate Mail Flies Through Cyberspace Jewish Groups Seek Answers and Action." *Jewish Telegraphic Agency* (20 December): 7.

Turner, Victor. 1967. *The Forest of Symbols: Aspects of Ndembu Ritual*. Ithaca, N.Y.: Cornell University Press.

———. 1969. *The Ritual Process: Structure and Anti-Structure*. Chicago: Aldine.

———. 1974. *Dramas, Fields, and Metaphors*. Ithaca, N.Y.: Cornell University Press.

———. 1977. "Variations on a Theme of Liminality," pp. 36–52 in *Secular Ritual*. Edited by Sally F. Moore and Barbara G. Myerhoff. Amsterdam, The Netherlands: Van Gorcum, Assen.

———. 1979. *Process, Performance and Pilgrimage: A Study in Comparative Symbology*. New Delhi, India: Concept Publishing.

———. 1982a. *From Ritual to Theater: The Human Seriousness of Play*. New York: Performing Arts Journal Publications.

———, ed. 1982b. *Celebration: Studies in Festivity and Ritual*. Washington, D.C.: Smithsonian Institution.

Turner, Victor, and Edith Turner. 1978. *Image and Pilgrimage in Christian Culture: Anthropological Perspectives*. New York: Columbia University.

Tuttle, William M., Jr. 1977. *Race Riot: Chicago in the Red Summer of 1919*. New York: Atheneum.

Van Gennep, Arnold. 1960. *The Rites of Passage*. Translated by Monika B. Vizedom and Gabrielle L. Caffee. Chicago: University of Chicago Press.

Vaughn, Diane. 1983. "Uncoupling: The Social Construction of Divorce," pp. 405–22 in *Social Interaction: Readings in Sociology*. Edited by H. Robboy and C. Clark. New York: St. Martin's.

———. 1986. *Uncoupling: Turning Points in Intimate Relationships*. New York: Oxford University Press.

Veblen, Thorsten. 1899. *Theory of the Leisure Class*. New York: Macmillan.

Velez-Ibanez, Carlos G. 1993. "Ritual Cycles of Exchange: The Process of Cultural Creation and Management in the U.S. Borderlands," pp. 119–39 in *Celebrations of Identity: Multiple Voices in American Ritual Performance*. Edited by Pamela R. Frese. Westport, Conn.: Bergin & Garvey.

Vinge, Joan. 1985. "An Open Letter to Andre Norton," pp. 1–3 in *Moonsinger's Friends*. Edited by Susan Schwartz. New York: Bluejay.

Vizedom, Monika. 1976. *Rites and Relationships: Rites of Passage and Contemporary Anthropology*. Beverly Hills, Calif.: Sage.

Wallace, Mike. 1985. "Mickey Mouse History: Portraying the Past at Disney World." *Radical History Review* #32: 33–57.

Warren, Stacy. 1994. "Disneyfication of the Metropolis: Popular Resistance in Seattle." *Journal of Urban Affairs* 16 (2): 89–107.

Weber, Max. 1958/1920. *Protestant Ethic and the Spirit of Capitalism*. Translation and Introduction by Talcott Parsons and Foreword by R. H. Tawney. New York: Scribner's.

Weiss, Robert S. 1975. *Marital Separation: Managing after a Marriage Ends*. New York: Basic Books.

Wells (-Barnett), Ida B. 1970. *Crusade for Justice: The Autobiography of Ida B. Wells*. Edited by Alfreda M. Duster. Chicago: University of Chicago Press.

West, John O. 1988. *Mexican-American Folklore: Legends, Songs, Festivals, Proverbs, Crafts, Tales of Saints, of Revolutionaries, and More*. Little Rock, Ark.: August House.

Whyte, William Foote. 1961. *Street Corner Society: The Social Structure of an Italian Slum*. Chicago: University of Chicago Press.

Williams, Norma. 1990. *The Mexican American Family: Tradition and Change*. New York: General Hall.

Willis, Susan. 1995. "The Family Vacation," pp. 34–53 in *Inside the Mouse* by the Project on Disney. Durham, N.C.: Duke University Press.

Wilson, Howard Eugene. 1927. *Mary McDowell and Her Work as Head Resident of the University of Chicago Settlement House, 1894–1904*. M.A. thesis, Department of History, University of Chicago.

———. 1928. *Mary McDowell: Neighbor*. Chicago: University of Chicago Press.

Yoke, Carl B. 1991. "Slaying the Dragon Within: Andre Norton's Female Heroes." *Journal of the Fantastic in the Arts* 4 (3): 79–92.

Young, T. R., and Garth Massey. 1978. "The Dramaturgical Society: A Macro-Analytic Approach to Dramaturgical Analysis." *Qualitative Sociology* 1 (September): 78–98.

Young, T. R., and John F. Walsh, eds. 1984. *Critical Dramaturgy*. Red Feather, Colo.: Red Feather Institute.

Zukin, Sharon. 1991. *Landscapes of Power: From Detroit to Disney*. Berkeley: University of California Press.

Index

About the Contributors

YOCHANAN ALTMAN is permanent visiting professor at the Institute of Business Administration, Université Jean Moulin-Lyon 3. He is the editor of the *Journal of Managerial Psychology* and associate editor-Europe of *Human Resources Development International*. He specializes in international and cross-cultural issues pertaining to management and organizations. A prolific author, he has recently published *Comparative Management* (1996) and *Careers in the Millennium* (1997). He earned his bachelor's and master's degrees from Bar-Ilan University, Israel, and his doctorate from Middlesex University, England.

MICHAEL R. BALL received his doctorate in sociology from the University of Nebraska-Lincoln. He has taught there, at the University of Nebraska-Omaha, and at the Beijing Teachers' College. He has studied and published in the areas of sociological history and theory, race and ethnic relations, and teaching sociology. His book, *Professional Wrestling as Dramatic Ritual in American Popular Culture* (1990), was translated into Japanese (1993). It explores popular culture from a ritual activities approach. He is currently Associate Professor of Sociology at the University of Wisconsin-Superior.

ANTHONY J. BLASI teaches sociology at Tennessee State University and completed a Ph.D. in sociology from the University of Notre Dame and a Th.D. in ethics from Regis College (Toronto) and the University of

Toronto. He has written extensively in sociological theory and in the sociology of music, ethics, and religion. His latest books are *Making Charisma, The Social Construction of Paul's Public Image* (1991), and *A Sociology of Johannine Christianity* (1997).

THOMAS C. CALHOUN is an Associate Professor of Sociology at the University of Nebraska-Lincoln. He is interested in researching drugs and religion as they impact the African-American community and juvenile male prostitution. His works appear in *Deviant Behavior, Sociological Inquiry, Sociological Spectrum, Journal of Social Psychology*, and the *Western Journal of Black Studies*.

JULIE ANN HARMS CANNON is a Visiting Assistant Professor of Sociology at the University of Nebraska-Lincoln. She received her B.A. in sociology from Western Washington University, Bellingham, Washington, and her M.A. and Ph.D. in sociology from the University of Nebraska-Lincoln. Her areas of specialization include sex and gender and sociological theory. She is currently developing a textbook on the women founders of sociological theory.

MARY JO DEEGAN is Professor of Sociology at the University of Nebraska-Lincoln. Her research interests include theory, methods, women, disability, and the history of the discipline. She received her Ph.D. in sociology from the University of Chicago where she was a member of Victor Turner's theory seminar and studied with Odin Anderson, Mercea Eliade, Victor Lidz, and Talcott Parsons, among others. She has published over 80 articles and chapters and numerous books, including *Jane Addams and the Men of the Chicago School, 1892–1918* (1988); *American Ritual Dramas* (Greenwood, 1989); and coedited the anthologies *Women and Disability* (1985), *Feminist Ethics and Social Science Research* (1989), and *Women in Sociology* (Greenwood, 1991).

RHONDA FISHER is an Assistant Professor of Sociology at Midland Lutheran College and a Ph.D. candidate in sociology at the University of Nebraska-Lincoln. She received her M.A.E. from Wayne State College, Wayne, Nebraska. Her research interests include Protestant Fundamentalism and violence, special-needs adoption, and deviance and gender.

SHARON K. LARSON is a doctoral student at the University of Nebraska-Lincoln, Department of Sociology. Her master's thesis dealt with cultural and structural impacts on rural-urban health differences. Sharon writes on a variety of topics often combining her 15 years of medical and teaching experience with her sociological interests. Forthcoming publications include several articles addressing women's health, history of the nineteenth amendment, women and adoption, parenting from a woman's perspective, and women in health careers. She is also currently involved in research on adoption issues and outcomes.

LISA K. NIELSEN is a master's candidate in the School of Journalism at the University of Nebraska-Lincoln. Her areas of specialization include business and management.

AGNES RIEDMANN is an Assistant Professor of Sociology at California State University-Stanislaus. She earned her master's degree from the University of Nebraska-Omaha and her doctorate from the University of Nebraska-Lincoln. She received her B.A. in Sociology from Creighton University. She has held teaching positions at the University of Nebraska-Lincoln and Creighton University and has had advanced research training in Australia. Her areas of specialization are the family, the sociology of literature, and methodology. She has coauthored several editions of *Marriage and Families: Making Choices and Facing Change*.

TODD J. SCHROER is finishing his doctoral studies at the University of Nebraska-Lincoln. His areas of specialization include social movements, criminology, and cultural studies, and he has presented papers on these topics at a number of national conferences. Through his ongoing studies he has become a leading expert on the white supremacist movement in America and how it is influenced by technological changes.

BERT WATTERS has held various positions in management and is a master's student at the University of Nebraska-Lincoln.

ISBN 0-313-30465-3

HARDCOVER BAR CODE